THE American CAR DEALERSHIP

ROBERT GENAT

MBI Publishing Company

DEDICATION

To George and Elaine Bohn

First published in 1999 by MBI Publishing Company, 729 Prospect Avenue, PO Box 1, Osceola, WI 54020-0001USA

© Robert Genat, 1999

MBI Publishing Company books are also available at discounts in bulk quantity for industrial or sales-promotional use. For details write to Special Sales Manager at Motorbooks International Wholesalers & Distributors, 729 Prospect Avenue, PO Box 1, Osceola WI, 54020 USA.

Library of Congress Cataloging-in-Publication Data

Genat, Robert.
        The American car dealership / Robert Genat.
                p. cm.
        Includes index.
        ISBN 0-7603-0639-7 (hardbound : alk. paper)
        1. Automobile dealers–United States–History. 2. Selling–
        Automobiles–United States–History 3. Automobile industry and
        trade–United States–History. I. Title.
HD9710.U52G359   1999
381'.456292'0973–dc21   99-32654

On the front cover: What could epitomize a car dealership better than a showroom and side lot full of brand-new 1957 Chevrolets? The 1950s not only brought glitz and chrome to the cars, but also to the very buildings from which they were sold and serviced.

On the frontispiece: For decades, Pontiac's Indian head identified cars and dealerships. Practically every Pontiac dealer—no matter how small—had a neon sign hanging outside its building to lure new customers. *Howard Ande*

On the title page: For almost a century, used car lots have been the place where first car dreams come true. Reasonable prices and a good selection of quality cars have been hallmarks of the reputable used car business. *Copyright © 1978–1999 GM Corp. Used with permission of GM Media Archives*

On the back cover: Car dealerships have been a part of the American roadside landscape for 100 years. From the top: an early 1930s showroom filled with new Auburns, Cords, and Duesenbergs *Auburn Cord Duesenberg Museum*, a neon-drenched Chevrolet dealership in 1963 *Copyright © 1978–1999 GM Corp. Used with permission of GM Media Archives*, a friendly used car dealer in the 1950s *Norm Kraus collection*, and a young couple taking delivery of their first new car, a 1960 Pontiac. *Copyright © 1978–1999 GM Corp. Used with permission of GM Media Archives*

Edited by Keith Mathiowetz
Designed by Tom Heffron

Printed in Hong Kong

CONTENTS

ACKNOWLEDGMENTS

Thanks go to Julia Daniel at the General Motors Archives and to Dan Hubbert at Chevrolet Public Relations. Thanks to the nice people at the Ford Motor Archives: Elizabeth Adkins, Darleen Flaherty, Pamela Przywara, and Michelle Blomberg. Special thanks go to John Emery at the Auburn-Cord-Dusenberg Museum and to Mark Patrick at the Detroit Public Library. Thanks to Wendy Barker and her staff at the Escondido, California, Historical Society. Thanks to Vicki Cwiok at the Sears Archives.

Thanks to the following people for their many and varied contributions: Dan Burger, Bob LaBonte, Terry Charmichael, Gary Jankowski, Vic Schneider, Tom Szott, Ken Stevens, Charlie DiBari, Joe Veraldi, Mickey Kress, Tom Geiman, David Warfield, Norm Kraus, Homer Gordon, Nick Koroly, associates at the Franklin D. Roosevelt Library, Ken Swift, Jim Wangers, Shelly Cleaver, Richard Bowman, Denny Williams, Dennis Cook, Dan Belt, Brad Joseph, Charles Tator, Mike Holland, Richard Newman, Hugh Gordon, Jennifer Wohletz, Martin Jack Rosenblum, Howard Ande, Helen J. Earley at the Oldsmobile Historical Center, Marc Stertz at NADA, Larry Weiner and Mary Agnes Davis. And thank you, Jeff Creighton, for coming up with the idea and for encouraging me to pursue it.

— Robert Genat

INTRODUCTION

In the last century, nearly 3,000 different automobile nameplates were sold in the United States, which is an amazing statistic. Many manufacturers built only one or two cars, while others were able to fight the larger manufacturers for decades before collapsing. Throughout the years, car dealers, with their love of selling automobiles, played key roles in the success of manufacturers.

In order to appreciate the role played by the auto dealer, an understanding of the evolution of the auto industry is necessary. Part of that understanding includes an appreciation of the ways in which cultural, historical, political, and economic changes affected the auto industry, as well as the car-buying public. These influential points governed not only the industry, but the methods used by dealers to sell cars as well.

One hundred years ago, the direction of the auto industry was uncharted territory to be explored by many people. In the late 1800s, automobile builders fell into one of two broad categories: the backyard mechanics who tinkered with engines and simply adapted them to a horse-drawn carriage, and the machinists and bicycle mechanics who understood drives and gearing. These inventors built the most advanced machines and set the stage for the development of the automobile as we know it today.

In 1879, George B. Selden was the first to apply for a patent for an automobile powered by a gasoline engine. Along with William Gomm, who designed and built a three-cylinder engine, Selden assembled a machine that would eventually change the face of American life. At that time, gasoline engine development was in its infancy, and gasoline was not a readily available product. Another aspect of gasoline engines was the strong arm required to start them. In the initial

stages of their development, gasoline engines created a deafening racket as well.

Other builders of the era relied on dependable battery electric power. Electric power was clean, quiet, and, at the turn of the century, drove 38 percent of the automobiles on the road. Steam was another power source that provided plenty of torque, but it lacked practicality because of the time required to build a fire to heat the water used in steam-powered cars. Steam cars also required a high level of maintenance.

The future of the gasoline automobile was secured in 1901, when new oil fields were discovered in East Texas. Gasoline had previously been considered a waste product of the oil refinement process. It had been used for household lighting, but its volatility had made it too dangerous to gain widespread favor. In 1900, annual domestic crude oil production was only 60 million barrels. With the discovery of new oil fields, and the emerging automobile market, oil production more than tripled in the next decade. During this period, large oil reserves and a plentiful supply of gasoline fed the rapid development of the gasoline engine.

By 1910 serious concerns arose regarding oil and gasoline demands of the automobile, which some felt might soon outstrip production. Within a few years, those concerns led to a doubling of the price of gasoline to nearly

17 cents a gallon from its previous level at 9.5 cents a gallon. To cope with the growing demands, new efficiencies in the oil refinement process soon increased the amount of gasoline that could be extracted from the crude oil.

The first documented sale of an American-built, gasoline-powered automobile took place on March 24, 1898, when Robert Allison purchased a Winton for $1,000. The Winton Motor Carriage Company, the sixth U.S. automobile manufacturer to produce a gasoline-powered vehicle, was founded by Alexander Winton, an immigrant from Scotland. Winton had a strong technical background that included a stint as a steamship engineer and a position as a superintendent at the Phoenix Iron Works in Cleveland, Ohio, in 1884. In 1890, however, Winton started his own company to manufacturer bicycle components, many of which he had invented himself. In 1891 he began manufacturing complete bicycles.

Winton was fascinated by the new automobiles and began experimenting with one in 1893. By 1896 he had a workable, gasoline-powered automobile, and in 1897 ceased bicycle production to focus on automobiles. Within five years, Winton was the largest automobile producer in the United States, turning out six cars a day. Winton was known as an experimenter and an excellent engineer, and even though he had more

Many early car dealers grew out of existing garages. The owners found that in addition to repairing cars, money could be made by selling them, too. The Escondido Garage sold Cadillac, Ford, and Reo. *Escondido Historical Society*

In 1910, Auburn was one of the many manufacturers in the automobile business. At that time, their cars, like so many others, were assembled from purchased components. Most dealerships of this era were located in small, unattractive buildings. This one is an exception.
Auburn Cord Duesenberg Museum

Detroit coal dealer, and on June 16, 1903, the Ford Motor Company was formed.

During the first decade of the twentieth century, many of the early experimenters fell by the wayside. The survivors were those who concentrated solely on automobiles. In the beginning, the making of cars was almost entirely an assembly process done with parts purchased from many different suppliers. Each automobile was assembled from start to finish, one car at a time.

Then in 1908, Henry Ford introduced the Model T and was quickly on his way to becoming the most prolific automobile manufacturer in America. In January of 1910, Ford's Highland Park, Michigan, plant opened, where, in 1913, the concept of the assembly line became a reality. The numbers tell the tale. In 1907, Ford built 8,000 Model N automobiles (the Model T's predecessor) for a profit of $1 million. In 1914, the first full year of the assembly line, Ford produced 250,000 Model T automobiles and a staggering $27 million profit.

In 1914, Henry Ford shocked the world with his decision to pay Ford Motor Company workers an unprecedented $5 a day (twice the average daily wage for an auto worker). No one but old Henry himself will ever know exactly why he did it. Ford had been seen as the champion of the ordinary man and his monetary decision elevated his status and captured the imagination of the public. The wage hike may have been an attempt to stem the high turnover rates of his workforce and a fear of the pressure to unionize from the International Workers of the World.

With this single stroke of generosity, Ford forever changed the face of American consumerism. Up until 1914, the automobile had been seen as transportation only for the rich. The average worker didn't have the income to buy an automobile. With the advent of the assembly line and the resulting lower cost of production, however, the Model T sold for less than $400 in 1916, making it affordable for the blue collar workers who were building it.

Ford also shared his profits with his customers and introduced the rebate. In a moment of marketing genius, Ford announced that if the company sold 300,000 automobiles between August 1, 1914, and August 1, 1915, he would give each buyer $50.

Auto production in 1915 was led by Ford Motor Company at 501,462 units—more than five times the production of the nearest competitor, Willys-Overland. More than half the automobiles made in the world were manufactured by Ford Motor Company. Truck production tripled over the previous year's level; much of the production increase was due to the the demand for equipment to fight World War I. By 1918, motor vehicle

than 100 patents to his name, he was a poor businessman. The Winton Corporation went out of business shortly after World War I.

Another notable innovator, Henry Ford, was a farm boy who went to the big city and made history. Ford's background in farm machinery and his inquisitive mind made him the equal of his automotive contemporaries. He served his apprenticeship in James Flower's Detroit, Michigan, machine shop, where he became an accomplished machinist. He also repaired watches to supplement his income, which led him to the idea of mass producing low-cost watches. This concept of a low-cost, high-production consumer item would reappear in Ford's future.

While working as an engineer at the Edison Illuminating Company, Henry Ford completed his first car—the Quadricycle—on June 4, 1896, at his shop on Detroit's Bagley Avenue. With its steel tube frame and large spoked wheels, the Quadricycle owed much of its design heritage to the bicycle, and at 500 pounds it was also the lightest of the early automobiles.

In 1899 Ford went into partnership with William Murphy to form the Detroit Automobile Company. This venture failed within a year, but they reorganized into a new entity named the Henry Ford Company, which also failed within a short period of time. Murphy criticized Ford for spending too much time racing. The pair split and Ford found a new partner, Alexander Malcomson, a registrations exceeded 5 million. All these astronomical figures were due, in large part, to the introduction of the assembly line.

Between 1914 and 1917, the output of automobiles in America jumped from 573,000 to 1.9 million. Car ownership became a realistic aspiration for almost every consumer. Ford dominated the low-price, entry-level models; and for most families, the Model T was their first car. For those wanting to move up in the automotive world, they could choose among the medium-priced Willys-Overland, Buick, Chevrolet, or Dodge, most of which could be purchased through time-payment offered by the companies.

Second only to the introduction of the assembly line, financing of car sales was probably the most significant step in the growth of the automobile industry. The General Motors Acceptance Corporation, formed in 1919 to provide financing for automobile sales, took the burden of financing automobile purchases from the shoulders of the individual dealers. So successful was GMAC financing that by 1922, more than 70 percent of the cars sold were purchased with some sort of financing. Henry Ford disapproved of financing until he devised his own plan in 1923, which featured weekly installments of $5.

As part of growing consumer interest in owning automobiles, General Motor's annual model changes quickly diminished the shine on the Model T. On May 31, 1927, the last of more than 15 million Model Ts built during its 19 years in production rolled off the assembly line. The Ford production line was then shut down in 1927 between May and December, at a cost of $250 million, to retool the plant for production of the new Model A.

Within the first two days of the new Model A's unveiling, an estimated 10 million people came out to see it. It was a good car, equal to, but not superior to its competitors. The new Model A could be bought in a variety of colors and in two-tone shades, since Ford's well-known practice of painting all of his cars black had ended in the mid 1920s. Two-year production totals of the Model A would hit 2 million units in July 1929, making it a banner year for the entire auto industry, which marked total production at just under 4.5 million units.

The Roaring Twenties fostered an automotive culture. The automobile had shifted from a frivolous possession of the rich to a necessity for the masses. In towns across the country, car dealerships, gas stations, roadside stands, and tourist camps sprang up, including the first drive-in restaurant in Dallas, Texas, in 1921. Closed-body sedans and coupes soon displaced open roadsters as the most popular body style, which allowed people to

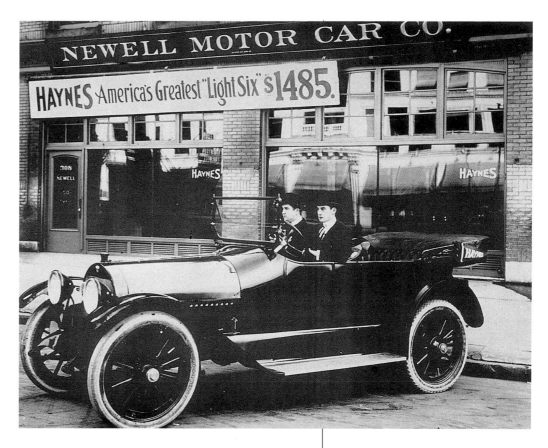

drive in inclement weather. Heaters were also installed to permit winter driving.

But the good times ended with the stock market crash on October 29, 1929, which plunged the country into a deep economic depression. By 1933, unemployment was five times the level of 1929. And even though motor vehicle production plummeted 75 percent between 1929 and 1933, strangely enough, automobile registrations dropped only 10 percent. The automobile was firmly rooted in American culture, clearly evidenced in the 1940 movie *The Grapes of Wrath*. Foreign moviegoers were amazed by the fact that even the poorest of Americans drove cars, even if they were only broken-down jalopies. American cowboy philosopher Will Rogers observed during the Depression that the United States was the only country where a person could drive himself to the poorhouse in an automobile.

In 1932, domestic auto production reached its lowest point since 1918, and the used car rose to prominence. One government agency even suggested scrapping more than 250,000 older cars to combat the used car problem. The depression proved to be tough on the smaller automakers, with more than 40 forced out of business. At the same time, the remaining manufacturers were trying to decide whether to cut prices on existing

Between 1900 and 1930, the American automobile business was built by tinkerers and visionaries. Car manufacturers were opening and closing at a rapid rate. Some produced only a few models before closing their doors. The manufacturer of the Haynes (parked here in front of franchise dealer Newell Motor Car Company) survived until 1925.

Henry Ford was one of the few manufacturers who realized that a strong dealer network was the key to surviving in the automotive business. By the late 1920s, the automobile had become a permanent part of American culture. An automobile franchise with a major manufacturer like Ford ensured a steady income, not only from car sales, but also from parts and service.

models or chance the introduction of new models. In 1935, President Roosevelt stepped in and requested that new model introduction dates be moved back from January to November in order to help stabilize employment within the auto industry.

The automakers then began pursuing the notion of planned obsolescence, and vehicle styling improved considerably during the 1930s. Early models were boxy, but as the decade progressed, designers adopted the Art Deco and streamline styles that were then so popular in architecture and industrial design. Along with these more popular designs in the late 1930s, increased production for the war effort in Europe helped to lift the domestic economy out of the Great Depression.

In 1941, Detroit went to war like the rest of the nation. By 1942, all wartime production of civilian cars ceased, and each of the manufacturers turned to defense production. Packard had already been producing aircraft engines since 1940, which made its wartime conversion smooth. More than 650,000 four-wheel drive Jeeps were produced by Ford and Willys. American Bantam, the company that designed the Jeep, also built fire pumper equipment. Chrysler built aircraft engines, radar units, Sherman tanks, and rockets. General Motors built everything from aircraft to anti-aircraft

guns. Ford Motor Company built 8,685 B-24 Liberators, the largest single model aircraft in production during the war. Ford also built tanks, armored personnel carriers, and gliders. Hudson, Nash, and Studebaker were also large wartime suppliers of defense goods.

Many of the cars produced in 1942 were purchased by the government for official use. In addition to the gas and tire rationing that was imposed for the duration of the war in an effort to conserve fuel, the national speed limit was set at 40 miles per hour and then later dropped to 35 miles per hour. It was difficult to get a car repaired during the war because automotive parts were rationed with a majority going for defense needs. Many of the mechanics who had worked at the dealerships were now overseas repairing aircraft or tanks instead of passenger cars.

Following the war, the pent-up demand for automobiles stemmed from several sources. Many of the older cars had just worn out. Men returning from war wanted to buy new cars, as did so many of the people who had worked on the war effort stateside. But the conversion of defense plants back to automobile production was difficult. Materials needed were in short supply and factories had to be retooled for production. The transition from war to peace was easiest for General Motors. GM was a flexible organization with diversity among its manufacturing facilities. For some of the same reasons, Chrysler made a smooth transition. Ford Motor Company struggled. The death of Henry Ford's son Edsel, and his decidedly antiquated business practices meant that Henry Ford and his company were in disarray. Henry Ford II was discharged early from the Navy to take over the helm of the company. He brought in the "Whiz Kids"—a group of highly touted business experts—to help with the transition and to boost the company's flagging finances.

The postwar era was a boon to the small producers who quickly converted back to auto production. Studebaker was the first to come out with a model that was significantly different from those produced in 1942. Entrepreneurs who had made a lot of money in the defense industry during the war decided to get in on the action in the automotive market. Henry Kaiser and Preston Tucker were the two most famous postwar car builders.

Americans continued their love affair with the car as each new model was released with sleeker styling and more voluptuous curves. In 1949, industry production hit a new high with 6,253,651 cars rolling off the assembly line. General Motors took the styling lead with new Chevys, Pontiacs, Buicks, and Oldsmobiles. GM's pillarless Buick and Oldsmobile hardtops and overhead valve V-8s gave General Motors a distinct edge over its competition. Chrysler's styling took a more conservative line, and Ford produced nicely crafted new models. With so many new features to see, the large auto shows were successful in whetting the public's appetite for new cars.

The car-buying frenzy continued into 1950. It was accelerated by U.S. involvement in the Korean conflict; fears of another car-buying drought drove customers to the showrooms. The auto manufacturers had to once again gear up for war, but this time on a much smaller scale. Demands of the war created shortages of certain critical raw materials, but auto sales continued to climb. In 1950, 39.6 million passenger cars were on the road, an increase of 40 percent from 1941.

In 1952, V-8 engines were standard in one-third of all cars manufactured. Automatic transmissions were installed in almost half of the new car production. New gadgetry, such as power steering, power seats, and power windows, caught the public's fancy. The Korean War ended on July 26, 1953, and with it ended many of the restrictions placed on the automotive industry. Ford and Chevrolet squared off in a selling war, where the factories forced cars on the dealers. General Motor's Motorama toured for six months displaying their dream cars to 1.7 million visitors.

The sales blitz of 1952 was the death knell to many small or fledgling automakers. The biggest obstacle for these smaller manufacturers was marketing their product.

Most had adequate engineering and manufacturing facilities, but they lacked an extensive dealer network to ensure ongoing sales. Successful dealers were not about to sever their ties with a major manufacturer to go with a company that was small, new, or speculative. The American automobile consumer also resisted buying a vehicle that was too different from the mainstream look.

You can almost imagine the salesman behind the wheel turning to his two passengers and saying, "So Mr. Capone, how did you and Mr. Nitti like the ride of the new Pierce-Arrow?" Pierce-Arrows were one of the most luxurious and noble cars ever manufactured. The company was acquired (some say saved) by Studebaker in 1928. Studebaker also owned the Rockne, produced only in 1932 and 1933. The J. F. O'Connor Sales Company sold all three lines of cars.

The Depression of the early 1930s proved devastating for the marginally financed automakers. Dealerships for the top-selling cars survived the drought by virtue of their parts and service departments. By the late 1930s, new car sales were on the rise. The start of World War II halted auto production and the dealers were once again in survival mode. Used cars, parts sales, and service saved many, while others closed their doors. *From the collections of Henry Ford Museum & Greenfield Village and Ford Motor Company*

Nash survived the war years by building aircraft engines, munitions, and cargo trailers. Following the war, the management at Nash was smart enough to realize that the company couldn't survive unless they produced something different. In 1950 the Rambler was introduced. The banners on the front of this rural Nash dealership announce the arrival of the 1951 models. Out front is their stock of rather motley-looking used cars.
Escondido Historical Society

They were concerned that such a vehicle might not have sufficient future trade-in value.

By the mid 1950s, the horsepower race was in full swing. Styling was also at a peak, and every car produced had a distinctive look. Unfortunately, handling and braking did not progress as quickly. A vain attempt was made at selling safety, but the public wanted style and horsepower. Late in 1956, the National Automobile Show was held in New York's new Coliseum (the first show since 1940). The show featured the new 1957 models and was the first to be televised. It was an age of fins, glitter, and three-toned paint. This exuberance lasted until the end of the decade, when fins got out of control and a recession hit, severely slowing car sales. Chevrolet led car sales in 1958 with 1.14 million units sold. Ford came in second with 987,945 units. Overall volume however was down 31.4 percent from the previous year. Also in 1958, the Automobile Information Disclosure Act required all new cars to display a window sticker listing the make, model, serial number, and a suggested retail price. At the end of the decade, the effect of the small German Volkswagen was felt. To counter the VW, some Buick dealers sold the German-built Opel, and a few Pontiac dealers sold the British Vauxhall. Feeling the need to compete, the manufacturers went back to the drawing board to design their own small cars.

In 1960, America was solidly recovering from the recession of 1958 with a new feeling of optimism in the air and a youthful new president to exemplify that spirit. Even though the Cold War was far from over—and just offshore a Cuban dictator was rattling his sword—Americans still had a great deal of faith in the future. That faith translated into car sales and the sales of consumer goods. Eighty percent of all families owned an automobile, and the interstate highway system begun in the 1950s was growing again. The United States was a country on the move, and cars were the favorite mode of transportation. People were driving more for business, too. Fleet cars, typically sold at or below dealer cost, were sold through traditional dealerships and, to keep the factory happy, the dealer would comply, even though he was losing money. Factories soon stopped their fleet programs and placed each dealer in charge of his own fleet sales.

The small car invasion of the late 1950s was enough to force the Big Three into action. Each company had its own idea of what a small car should be. These small cars—Chevrolet's Corvair, Ford's Falcon, and Plymouth's Valiant—were not stunning sellers; the margins were lower than those of the big cars. At a time when gasoline was only 14 cents a gallon, it was hard to convince the public to buy economy cars.

The full-size car dominated sales in the early 1960s. Ford and Chevrolet battled for sales supremacy, with Chevrolet the overall winner for the decade. Ford and Chevrolet sold a combined total of 9 million cars between 1965 and 1966. The horsepower race that started in the late 1950s continued and grew throughout the 1960s. Factories supported race teams and even built special-purpose race cars, and dealers painted their names on the sides of cars running at the local tracks. When the cars won, these dealers saw immediate traffic in the showroom. Customers didn't always buy the highest performance engine, but they bought the image of performance seen on the track. Several dealers across the country specialized in high-performance sales and prospered because of it.

In 1964, two watershed cars were released: the Mustang and the GTO. Both caused a flood of excitement that carried to the end of the decade. The only somber note was Ralph Nader's diatribe against the auto industry, targeting the Corvair specifically. Seatbelts became standard equipment in the early 1960s, and, later, collapsible steering columns, revised interiors, and door guard beams became parts of the basic car. Insurance rates soon matched horsepower, however, effectively killing the muscle car era.

The Japanese manufacturers started to look at the U.S. automotive market more seriously in the 1960s. In 1960, the Toyopet was the first imported car from

Toyota. It was underpowered, had boxy styling, and was not taken seriously by the automotive press or by the manufacturers in Detroit. The same was true of all other Japanese imports.

The 1970s was a decade of disco and disappointment. The government was trying to recover from years of war in Vietnam and from the Watergate fiasco. The auto companies, burdened with new and tighter emission and safety regulations, turned out cars that were uninspired when compared to those of the previous 20 years. Then in the winter of 1973, everyone in America became aware of OPEC, the Organization of Petroleum Exporting Countries, when it doubled the price of oil to $3 a barrel and imposed an embargo on oil shipped to the United States, creating shortages of gasoline and home heating oil. The impact was devastating to the industrialized nations that depended on oil. Cars lined up for blocks waiting to fill up at gas stations. Years of cheap, plentiful gas had lulled Americans into thinking it would always be available. As gas prices rose, the national speed limit was reduced to 55 miles per hour. The increased cost of transportation affected everyone's lifestyle and pocketbook.

The demand for small fuel-efficient cars caught U.S. car dealers unprepared for the crisis. The Japanese cars, laughed at a decade earlier, were now highly sought after. During that decade, Asian car makers had steadily improved their product and were in a golden position to impress U.S. car buyers. As a result, Japanese and European car dealers sold out of every car they had, while U.S. dealers were saddled with big, gas-guzzling sedans.

By the summer of 1974 when the oil crisis had eased, Americans had grown accustomed to higher prices for gasoline and were willing to pay as long as it was available. The demand for large cars soon returned and, along with the oil crisis and new emission laws, put a great deal of pressure on the auto companies. The cost of doing business was rising and so were car prices. For example, during one five-year period during the 1970s, the price of cars doubled, and "sticker shock" became part of the American lexicon. In addition to much higher prices, the new cars were filled with uninspired features like tufted velour, opera windows, and vinyl tops. No wonder, then, that the more Americans looked at, owned, and drove domestic cars, the more they

In the mid 1950s, Packard was financially hurt by two events: their merger with Studebaker and the loss of Briggs as their supplier of bodies. The recession of 1958 brought the company to its knees and the once-proud marque was finished.

In 1960, each of the Big Three introduced a new compact car. Just inside the showroom to the left is Chevrolet's entry—the Corvair. The market presence of three new entries to the field applied pressure to small manufacturers like AMC and Studebaker and to the foreign threat headed by Volkswagen.

Copyright © 1978-1999 GM Corp. Used with permission of GM Media Archives

opted for imports. Adding to their somewhat negative image, a second fuel crisis at the end of the decade put domestic manufacturers into a tailspin.

Chrysler was hardest hit by the economic downturn. The cars they had available were not selling, and the cars that they had planned for the future were not going to sell. Chrysler needed a shot in the arm, which happened when Henry Ford II fired Lee Iacocca. Iacocca went to Chrysler and immediately circled the wagons and began work on the new K car. In an unprecedented move, he also went to the U.S. government for a loan to bail out the flagging automaker. The

K cars were a success, and they were followed up by Chrysler's new minivan.

The situation over at Ford Motor Company was also shaky. Ford, like Chrysler, needed a hot-selling car to remain competitive in the 1980s. In the late 1970s, Ford assembled a team of designers to develop a new mid-sized sedan. This car, the Taurus, would be the savior of Ford Motor Company. It had rounded styling and front-wheel drive. It was a breath of fresh air from a company that had been producing boxy, uninteresting cars. The Taurus became a symbol of Detroit's ability to do something right in the face of an import challenge.

At General Motors, Chairman Roger Smith went on a spending spree. He bought computer systems giant EDS and aerospace manufacturer Hughes. Smith spent millions of dollars on equipment to modernize plants. Unfortunately, without a plan in place to use the equipment. Smith's excessive capital spending was done at the cost of research and development on new cars. GM's cars all looked alike and were ridiculed in a television commercial for Lincoln. In that commercial, upon leaving a classy restaurant, a well-heeled couple asks the valet parking attendant for their Cadillac. As the couple climbs into the black sedan brought for them, another well-dressed gentleman says sheepishly, "Excuse me, I believe that's my Buick." The Cadillac owner asks the valet if the next car is his, but is told it's an Oldsmobile. Finally, another dapper couple walks out and asks for their Lincoln Town Car. As the car pulls up, the voice-over croons, "There's nothing like a Lincoln." As the Lincoln drives out of the frame, the mass of GM owners are left to sort out their look-alike Pontiacs, Buicks, Oldsmobiles, and Cadillacs.

The one bright spot for GM in the late 1980s was the creation of Saturn. Saturn was an entirely new car (the first in 30 years) that GM hoped would appeal to import buyers. Saturn dealers were unique. Their no-dicker price policy and excellent customer service established a new trend in car sales and manufacturing.

The latest headline of the U.S. automotive story was the release of Volkswagen's New Beetle. The New Beetle caught the imagination of those who fondly

remembered the original Beetle, and showrooms were jammed to see this newest incarnation of the fabled VW.

Cars and car-buying habits have changed over the years. In the early days, individuals sold cars on the front porch of their house. Today, we have mega-dealers and expansive auto parks where a thousand new cars can be seen. Additionally, the Internet is making an impact on the way Americans are buying cars. But the independent franchise automobile dealer will always be at the heart of the automotive business.

CHAPTER 1

THE CAR BUSINESS

RISK TAKERS AND VISIONARIES

In 1895, there were only four registered automobiles in the United States. Within five years, there were over 4,000 cars manufactured by dozens of automakers. Following the completion of these first cars, the next problem appeared: how do we market and sell these contraptions? The early motor carriages were initially sold from the factory and in factory-owned stores. These fledgling automakers tried every way possible to sell cars, including mail order, consignment, and even traveling salesmen. Soon it became clear that a better distribution system would be needed. The independent businessman-dealer was the answer. This system also provided much-needed capital to the manufacturers; the small businessmen ended up being the automakers' salvation.

In 1896, William Metzger of Detroit opened the first independent automobile dealership. The first car he sold was a Waverly electric, but he also sold several different makes of motor cars. That same year, the first franchise dealership of domestically produced cars was opened by H.O. Kohller in Reading, Pennsylvania, where he sold Winton motor vehicles. The genie was now out of the bottle. With dealers in place, the automobile was gaining widespread attention and acceptance.

In 1899 the trend continued when Percy Owen opened the first automobile showroom in New York City where he sold Winton cars. Also in 1899, the Back Bay Cycle and Motor Company of Boston added renting, sales, storage, and repair of motor vehicles to their bicycle business. The bicycle was the main business of John Willys. He added his own line of motorcars to the bicycles in his showroom. The Studebaker wagon company showrooms also carried the new Studebaker automobiles.

These early days in the automotive business were driven by entrepreneurs and visionaries. The early storefront dealerships soon grew into purpose-built auto showrooms and repair facilities. Because of the volatility in the unstable auto business, manufacturers came and went, as did the early dealers. To survive, many of the early dealers took on several makes to be confident of a steady supply of vehicles to sell. Often, the agreement to become a dealer was simply made with a handshake, a few dollars changing hands, and an agreement to accept two cars. In 1902, to increase consumer confidence in new automobiles, the National Association of Automobile Manufacturers, an organization with only 112 members at the time, adopted a 60-day guarantee on cars produced by members of their organization.

In 1905, cars were first sold on the installment plan. This made it easier for the consumer to afford this new expensive luxury. Also in 1905, two dealer groups formed, the National Association of Automobile Dealers and the Associated Garages of America. Both soon failed. In 1907 another attempt was made to organize the car dealers with the formation of the National Automobile Dealers Association of America. This organization, like its predecessors, would also fail. It wasn't until 1917 that a permanent organization, the National Association of Auto Dealers (NADA), was formed to effectively represent the then 15,000 automotive dealers.

Between 1900 and 1920, there were 600 manufacturers building cars, with most not surviving after one or two cars. Because of the transitory state of the auto business, banks were not inclined to loan money to a new automobile venture. Many of the people building cars were tinkerers with great mechanical ability, but no business skills. Because of the newness of their product, they had a difficult time raising cash to complete their projects. Even established automakers had a hard time raising the money they needed to survive.

The answer to the financing of continued manufacturing operations came with the independent auto dealers. These dealers sent the manufacturers large deposits on new cars which provided the funding for the continued operation of assembling cars. In those early years, selling cars was not difficult. The automobile caught the fancy of those who could afford this new means of transportation and they were willing to give dealers large deposits for the opportunity to buy a car. Through 1920, demand was continually higher than supply. Because the dealers were continually sending in orders with a cash deposit, the manufacturers left them alone and didn't require any type of detailed reports or sales forecasts.

For the most part, a franchise to sell new automobiles didn't cost anything to obtain. It was granted to a person, who in the manufacturer's estimation, would be a good representative of the company and its products. The contract

The new and used car sales areas of a dealership are called the "front end" of the business. The parts and service business are the "back end." It's an old adage in the car business that the front end gets the business, but the back end keeps the business.
Copyright © 1978-1999 GM Corp. Used with permission of GM Media Archives

was at most two pages of uncomplicated "legalese." The territory claimed by the franchisee was spelled out in detail and often a map of the area was attached to the contract. While giving the dealer a defined territory, it was not exclusive. The company retained the right to grant another franchise in that territory or to make sales in that territory from company stores (sales outlets owned by the manufacturer).

There were requirements in the contract to have a facility from which to sell and service the products represented. Proper signage was a requirement in order to identify the building as an authorized dealer.

Rules for the early dealers were simple—sign an agreement to sell cars, and a territory would be assigned. Most of these agreements required that the franchisee also stock spare parts and offer a repair service for the cars sold. The dealer was required to have an adequate supply of parts on hand for any repairs needed. A contract for a new Ford dealer in 1917 required the dealer to maintain a $20,000 inventory of parts at all times. The dealer received a 1/3 discount on all parts purchased from Ford. In addition to parts, the dealer was required to offer repair services to its customers and to any other Ford owner, even if the vehicle was purchased

In the early 1920s, H. O. Kennedy opened the first Dodge Brothers dealership in Marion, Ohio. Here, he can be seen on the right with the entire dealership staff and two new 1923 Dodge Brothers cars.
Robert Palmer collection

from another dealer. The dealer was required to keep at least one new model on hand at all times as a demonstrator. This was excellent logic on the company's part, because who would want to by something as exotic as an automobile without seeing one firsthand?

A down payment of 10 percent of the wholesale price was required from the dealer to the manufacturer to order a car. Most of the time, this money was received by the dealer from the customer placing the order. The balance was paid to the dealer when the car was delivered. A mechanical aptitude was necessary to be a dealer in the early 1900s. When the cars were shipped to the dealer from the manufacturer, they were only partially complete. They needed final assembly and quite often that was done at the train station where the cars arrived in boxcars.

Selling in another franchised dealer's territory was a serious breach of decorum. Most manufacturers felt it destroyed the organizational efficiency of the franchise dealer system. If a dealer was found to be selling in another dealer's territory, a fine would be levied for each car sold. If the violations continued, the dealer could lose his franchise.

Dealers were able to purchase new cars at discounts ranging from 10 to 25 percent. Discounting to retail customers was not encouraged; in fact, it was flatly discouraged. The manufacturers felt that discounting would lead to competition between dealers and cause dealers to sell outside their territory.

In addition to franchise car dealers, there were also factory stores. A factory store, also known as a branch store or branch dealer, was a dealership owned and run by the manufacturer. All of the employees were paid a salary directly by the manufacturer. Factory stores would always be a sore point for any independent businessman who had invested his life savings into a business and who worked hard for it to succeed. The factory stores had virtually unlimited funding from the company and a large staff of salaried workers. The major concern on the part of the independent dealers was the direct competition the factory stores gave to the franchise dealers. The managers of factory stores were often the Zone or Regional Managers for a prescribed territory. Independent dealers had to tread lightly around these managers, because their fate was in their hands. While the local manager may not have had the power to cancel a franchise (a power usually

With a total investment of $100, H. Deets Warfield opened his Chevrolet dealership in 1916. In addition to Chevrolets, Warfield sold Fordson farm equipment, gasoline, and did auto repairs. *David Warfield collection*

19

In 1914, D. E. Stetler opened his first dealership with borrowed money. In 1920, he moved into this new facility on Roosevelt Street in York, Pennsylvania. The Stetler family has kept the Dodge franchise alive for more than 80 years and still operates a dealership in York. *York Historical Society*

left to the manufacturer), he did have the ability to add another franchise to the territory or make life miserable for the independent.

In the early days, factory stores also performed another important function, that of vehicle assembly. The centrally located branch dealer would often be the location where all new cars for the area were shipped by rail. Factory trained mechanics would unpack and assemble the cars at the rail yard. The local area dealer mechanics would participate in the process to learn how the new cars were put together. Following assembly, they would help by driving the cars back to their home

dealerships. Mechanics were often needed to repair one of the new cars when it broke down on the trip from the train station to the new car dealership.

In those early years, manufacturers were always looking for someone qualified to be a dealer. In their advertising, the early auto companies promoted not only their cars, but a career as an auto dealer. At machinery and bicycle shows, company representatives would approach likely candidates and offer them a chance to become a franchised automobile dealer. It was at one of these shows that William "Billy" Hughson got involved in the auto business.

Hughson was born in Buffalo, New York, in 1869. The romantic tales of the Wild West enticed him to strike out for a new adventure. While still in his teens, he traveled to San Francisco to seek his fortune. Once there, he started working for a sales organization that represented many Eastern manufacturers. In 1902, his company sent him to Chicago to search for new products at a bicycle show. While at that show he came upon what appeared to be a four-wheeled bicycle. He struck up a conversation with the slender man demonstrating the machine. The gentleman explained to Hughson that what he was looking at was a motorized carriage, also known as an "automobile." A detailed description of the machine followed. Hughson attentively listened as the gentleman expounded upon his vision of the future of these machines. Following the presentation the gentleman, Henry Ford, introduced himself and then asked Hughson if he would be interested in selling his invention. Hughson thought a motor carriage was as good a commodity to sell as a bicycle and he shook hands with Ford and agreed to purchase $5,000 worth of automobiles as soon as production started.

Six months later, Hughson arrived in Detroit with his company's $5,000. He arrived in time to see the formation ceremonies of Ford Motor Company. Hughson's original deal was for automobiles, but Ford tried to convince him to invest the money into the company instead, since there were no cars available at that time. Hughson wired his partners and told them of the opportunity. The message he received back stated, "You went there to buy automobiles. Now, buy automobiles!" Following his company's instructions, Hughson purchased 12 automobiles making him Ford's first dealer. The fateful decision not to invest in Ford Motor Company was one that could have earned him and his partners millions upon millions of dollars.

Hughson's Ford automobiles sat unsold for three years. In the early 1900s, San Francisco was not the best place to sell cars. It lacked the sophistication of Eastern cites like New York. It also lacked developed roads. Occasionally one would be rented to a curious party, but for the most part, these cars were seen as rich man's toys.

A local tragedy would eventually change the public's perception of Hughson's cars. In 1906, an earthquake shook San Francisco, devastating the city. Hughson was confident that his fleet of automobiles could help rescuers. He, along with five other men, fought their way through the rubble of collapsed and burning buildings to the Market Street garage where his cars were stored. They drove six of the cars to safety. The six remaining cars were destroyed. Hughson turned his six cars over to the Red Cross for ambulance work. The rugged little Fords performed admirably, climbing steep hills where other vehicles failed.

As a reward for Hughson's contribution to the disaster relief, U.S. Army General Funston, who was in charge of reconstruction, made certain that Hughson's dealership office was the first business to be rebuilt on Market Street. Hughson's contribution to the relief effort also convinced the general population that the automobile was more than a folly. From that point on, Hughson's Ford dealership prospered.

Hughson's automotive dealership legacy is enormous. In his original agreement with Ford, he was given all of the West Coast territory, which included California, Oregon, Washington, Alaska, and Hawaii. At one time, there were 120 dealerships that could be traced directly to Hughson. Hughson also found and restored Henry Ford's 999 race car and presented it to Henry as a gift. Hughson Ford, the oldest Ford agency in America, closed its doors in July 1979, ten years after the death of its founder, Billy Hughson.

Business at Escondido, California's, Oscar Hall Ford has come to a halt while the annual Grape Day parade passes by. This large dealership offered full drive-through gas station services under the opening in the front of the building. The roots of this Ford dealership and many others on the West Coast are traceable to Billy Hughson. *Escondido Historical Society*

Chevrolet, which had its first full year of production in 1912, was also in need of dealers. By 1915, the company had branch sales offices in Oakland, California; Kansas City, Missouri; Atlanta, Georgia; St. Louis, Missouri; and Oshawa, Canada. With the release of their 490 model (so named because it cost $490) in 1916, Chevrolet production reached an all time high of 70,000 units. More dealers were needed, especially on the east coast.

A Chevrolet representative searching for new dealers in Maryland was told to talk to a young man by the

name of H. Deets Warfield. Warfield, a risk-taker with an entrepreneurial style, he jumped at the opportunity. "My grandfather had to put up $50 to get the franchise and purchase $50 worth of parts," says David Warfield. "He had $50, but had to borrow the other $50 from a local merchant who owned a general store." Warfield moved his dealership into a small two-bay building from which he also sold farm equipment.

The first Chevrolet Warfield sold was a 1917 model 490 touring car. The customer ordered it in the Winter with the stipulation that he wouldn't take

delivery until Spring. Warfield complied with the gentleman's request, storing the car in his father's buggy barn. When spring arrived the car was pulled out of storage and delivered. Three years later, the gentleman traded the model 490 for a new car and Warfield kept the 490. In fact, the family still owns it today and it's prominently displayed in the showroom of Damascus Chevrolet, in Damascus, Maryland.

Deets Warfield prospered in the auto business. At one time he owned four Chevrolet dealerships in Maryland. As his heath began to fail in 1953, he sold off all

but the Damascus dealership which his son, Deets Jr., was running at the time. In 1977 Deets Jr. turned the Damascus dealership over to his son David, who still runs the business today.

In the past, the job of a car salesman was the exclusive domain of white males. Ed Davis was an individual who figured out a way in, through hard work and diligence. Davis, born in 1911, showed an interest in cars at a young age. While working at a Dodge plant in Hamtramick, Michigan, in 1934, Davis' plant manager asked him if he would like to sell new cars part time to

In the early days of the automobile business, cars were available in all price ranges, from inexpensive transportation cars, like Ford and Chevy, to the more luxurious vehicles like these 1931 Auburns. Dealers found that they had to actively merchandise their product with a showroom full of cars and with displays that showed the inner workings of their offerings. *Auburn Cord Duesenberg Museum*

interview Davis said, "It was a matter of accepting a situation to achieve your objective. I didn't put it that way then, but I can put it that way now. As long as I was able to accomplish what I wanted and was selling more cars than they were, it didn't bother me too much. They were the ones worried about all the cars I was selling."

Davis also encountered problems with the service manager who was from the deep South. Whenever Davis sold a car, the service manager would park the car outside and not have it prepped for delivery. One day Davis asked the service manager about a car he had just sold and the manager sucker punched him, knocking out one of his teeth. Davis got up and returned the favor. They were both taken to the hospital by dealership owner, Lampkins. On the way back to the dealership, the service manager told Lampkins that he didn't like Davis and didn't want to work with him. Lampkins told the service manager that if he didn't work with Davis he wasn't going to have a job. The confrontation with the service manager proved to everyone in the dealership that Davis would not be pushed around and that he had the full support of the owner. Soon after, the service manager lost his job.

Davis developed a successful sales technique while working for Lampkins. In addition to the car the dealership gave him to drive, Davis bought an additional demonstrator–a brand new 1935 Plymouth– which cost him $497. Davis would carefully select the people to whom he gave the demonstrator, preferring to give it to church going families. He would let potential customers

In 1935, when this photo was taken, the country was fighting its way out of the Depression. Large dealerships like this Chevrolet agency had to make the most of every department in order to survive. *Copyright © 1978-1999 GM Corp. Used with permission of GM Media Archives*

the workers in the plant. This manager's son, Merton Lampkins, was opening his own Chrysler-Plymouth dealership and was looking for any sales he could get. Lampkins paid Davis $10 for each car he sold. Davis started selling so many cars while working at the plant that Lampkins offered him a full time position at the dealership. Unfortunately, Lampkin's all white sales staff refused to work with Davis. In an *Automotive News*

One of the benefits of a new car franchise is income derived from other profit centers that are part of the business. Traditionally, whenever new car sales slow down, the parts and service businesses increase. *Copyright © 1978-1999 GM Corp. Used with permission of GM Media Archives*

In May 1917, 30 automobile dealers met in Washington, D.C., to change the way the government viewed the automobile. This coalition of dealers was there to convince the lawmakers that the automobile was no longer a rich man's toy, but that cars were vital to the U.S. economy. These dealers were successful in preventing a complete conversion of all auto manufacturing facilities to defense factories during the war. They also convinced Congress to reduce the proposed luxury tax from 5 to 3 percent. Buoyed by their success, these dealers realized that the nation's auto dealers needed ongoing representation in Washington. In July, 130 dealer representatives met in Chicago to elect Milwaukee dealer George Browne as the first president of the National Automobile Dealers Association. Within two years, NADA sponsored the National Motor Vehicle Theft Law, which made it a federal crime to transport a stolen car across state lines. They were also active in seeking auto finance reforms. The rapidly expanding automobile dealership network now had some direction, and standards were being set that would help both dealers and car buyers.

In 1922, NADA began an extended study of used car values. Until this time, used car prices varied from dealer to dealer. In 1933, the first copy of NADA's Official Used Car Guide was shipped to 40,000 subscribers. The guide's 388 pages reflected up-to-date used car values for 21 regions of the country. Because of its accuracy, the Guide received the U.S. government's endorsement on used car values. Today NADA's Official Used Car Guide is the accepted bible for used car prices.

By 1934, NADA's membership totaled 30,000. Factory relations and profit margins took center stage throughout the 1930s. Throughout the era of Prohibition, NADA lobbied on behalf of dealers who suffered losses when cars on which they had unpaid liens were confiscated because the owners violated liquor laws. A standard used car appraisal form was created in 1936. Also at this time, NADA began a dealer education program on used car sales. The period from 1936 to 1942 was marked by many positive changes in the relationships between the auto manufacturers and the dealers.

NADA marked its 25th anniversary in 1942, one of the most difficult years for automobile dealers. A Census Bureau report stated that auto dealers were among the businesses that were hit the hardest by the war program. NADA worked to boost dealer morale and lobbied to minimize war-related rationing. In 1942 and 1943, NADA was asked to help recruit skilled mechanics for the war effort. NADA's 1943 convention was canceled because of a wartime ban on assemblies of more than 50 people. The first postwar convention was held in Atlantic City in 1947. A record 6,500 people attended the convention representing 32,000 member dealers. It was also in the late 1940s that NADA made the prediction that automobile advertising on the new medium of television would become a permanent sales tool for the industry.

In 1950, the postwar car-buying boom was quieted by production halts for the Korean War. NADA fought government-mandated price controls on cars and the 7 percent excise tax added to the price of each new car. It was also during the 1950s that NADA started a campaign urging dealers to adopt a code of ethics. Surveys showed that the public thought dealer profits were too high and that dealers were unethical.

The 1960s saw many federally mandated changes to automobiles that directly affected the dealer's selling and servicing practices. Gas shortages and the increase of import dealers were on the agenda throughout the 1970s.

Today NADA's membership exceeds 19,500 domestic and import dealers. The goals of the small group that met in 1917 remain the same for members today: to preserve the value of the franchise system, and to communicate dealer views to government agencies, manufacturers, and the public. NADA is also there to strengthen the financial position of its members by providing professional programs and services that improve member business skills.

For a franchise that combines a quality product, low prices, liberal factory policies and the "hottest" demonstration feature of the year . . .

Pontiac's the Answer!

WHEN YOU GO INTO BUSINESS it's sound sense to give yourself every possible break. And that's exactly what you do when you sign a Pontiac franchise.

You handle a product without a peer for quality. America calls Pontiac the most beautiful thing on wheels. People who ought to know have named it the most trouble-free car in the industry. And every feature is the finest money can buy. This all-around excellence, moreover, is widely known—so that you can list good will among your assets the day you open for business.

But quality alone is not enough. Even quality merchandise must be properly priced. And Pontiac is. The six is priced in the field where nearly 90 per cent of

all sales are made—*right down near the lowest*. And the eight is the lowest-priced in the General Motors line!

That's plenty—but it isn't all! You can plan on getting full return from this happy combination of quality and low price because dealer policies are liberal in the extreme. Sliding scale discounts, protected territories—whatever it takes to make money, the Pontiac contract provides.

These are the long-haul features of the franchise. In addition you get the thinking of an engineering staff which can be counted on to keep Pontiac in the limelight. Safety Shift*, for example, is the biggest advancement of 1938, and Pontiac is the only low-priced car to provide it!

Here is a money-making combination in anybody's language. Yet you have read just the highlights. If you're interested in detailed facts and in available territory, write to C.P. Simpson, General Sales Manager, Pontiac Motor Division, General Motors Sales Corporation, Pontiac, Michigan. All correspondence will be considered strictly confidential.

ONLY LOW-PRICED CAR WITH SAFETY SHIFT $10 *OPTIONAL*

Safety Shift Gear Control doubles driving ease and clears the front floor, yet there is nothing new to learn and nothing to get out of order. As the simplest, lowest-priced, remote control shift offered as optional equipment, it is far and away the finest demonstration feature of the year.

Almost all of the advertising for the first cars contained some mention of franchise ownership. Later, when economic times became tough, the manufacturers once again actively advertised for franchisees. Each of these three ads from the NADA Bulletin features its unique spin to attract new blood into the business.

keep the car for a weekend. The family would take the demonstrator to church, all of their friends would rave about the car, and then they had to have it.

In 1940, Davis became the first black to own a new car dealership. "It was difficult," says Davis. "But, almost everything I was doing no other blacks had done. I took the responsibility to make something happen that wasn't happening." Davis stayed with Studebaker until 1956, when the Studebaker nameplate died. In 1963, Davis once again broke new ground by being the first black to receive a Big Three franchise. On November 11, 1963, he opened Ed Davis Chrysler Plymouth. Davis ran that dealership until 1971 when he retired.

The end of World War I saw a sharp increase in the demand for new cars. Also at this time, the General Motors Acceptance Corporation was formed. Its function was to finance the dealers' purchase of vehicles. This enabled large quantities of vehicles to be shipped for display and sale. As the Jazz Age dawned, the National Automobile Chamber of Commerce predicted that auto sales in 1920 would reach 3.5 million units. Installment buying of automobiles was initiated in 1910, but it took a decade to catch on. The demand for cars tapered off by July, 1920, and production totaled a little under 2 million for that year. With sales down, the manufacturers had a difficult time holding prices. Raw material costs remained high and reduced production cut into profits. Sales continued to decline and many manufacturers temporarily closed their doors. Even the mighty Ford Motor Company halted production for a short period. The parts business was still brisk and this gave the manufacturers enough working capital to continue.

In 1921, Ford Motor Company took a hard line regarding the economic slowdown and its dealer network suffered. Newly appointed sales

manager William Ryan informed all dealers that their sacred sales territories were eliminated. Ryan put a positive spin on the plan by stating that it would allow all dealers to expand and reach out into new territory. Ford felt that the protected territories gave each dealer a captive market, encouraging complacency rather than hustling for new sales.

Ford's restructuring plan did not spur sales as he had hoped. His next plan would once again place the dealers in a vice. Totally ignoring the stagnate sales climate, he started shipping cars to dealers at the rate he had the year before. When the cars arrived at the dealership, the owner was required to pay for the cars or risk losing the Ford Franchise. Ford Motor did help the dealers secure financing for the cars shipped. The practice of shipping cars that dealers had not ordered was carried out not only by Ford Motor Company, but by many other manufacturers to help them through tough economic times.

Now—even greater opportunity from the
FORD FRANCHISE

• The *new* Ford Dealer Franchise offers *the broadest opportunities of any single franchise in the automobile industry.* Today, a Ford dealership is indeed headquarters for automobile transportation.

The Ford dealer is in better position to handle the transportation needs of every owner, or prospective owner, in the territory he serves because he can offer the most complete line of merchandise of any automobile dealer in the industry.

Best of all, there's no overlapping competition within the Ford line.

Ford, Mercury, Lincoln-Zephyr and Lincoln—each car is in a clean-cut price class all its own—a complete line of quality-built automobiles.

Backed by a large advertising investment and aggressive, progressive sales policies, the *new* Ford Dealer Franchise represents a real opportunity for the right man in the right territory.

For full information on opportunities available at this time, consult the nearest Ford Branch—or write direct to Sales Department, Ford Motor Company, Dearborn, Michigan.

FORD MOTOR COMPANY
FORD, MERCURY, LINCOLN-ZEPHYR AND LINCOLN MOTOR CARS
AND FORD TRUCKS AND COMMERCIAL CARS

During World War II, many dealerships closed their doors because no new cars were being produced. The lack of new car production required the older ones to be maintained. Many dealers focused on used cars, parts, and service to survive the war years. These well-established dealers enjoyed the long-awaited car-buying boom of the postwar years. *Detroit Public Library, The National Automotive History Collection*

DODGE
1924 GREETS 1948

In 1913, under the direction of James Couzens, Ford Motor Company had 7,000 dealers selling the Model T. Ford's large size not only gave them the ability to manufacture cars efficiently and with less expense, but they could also afford a much larger sales force. The larger sales force was able to reach more customers. Smaller automakers were now beginning to feel the pinch and each year more and more would close their doors.

World War II created an especially severe hardship on automobile dealers. The manufacture and delivery of new models was halted in early 1942. Virtually all manufacturing facilities used to produce cars were converted to the production of defense goods. Without a supply of new cars, many dealerships simply closed their doors. Others focused on the used car business and parts and service. Douglas Chevrolet in High Springs, Florida, combined the dealership with a feed store and even sold groceries. Other dealerships converted their shop areas into small manufacturing facilities for war goods. Patriotism was high and many of the young men working in the dealerships dropped their grease guns and wrenches

and volunteered for military service. This created job openings that were soon filled by women. Rosie the Riviter's sister was doing her part by keeping America mobile working on the grease rack and changing spark plugs.

When auto production resumed at the end of the war, the 1946 models delivered to the dealerships were warmed-over 1942 models. It wouldn't be until 1949 that the auto industry would have anything new to show the car-hungry American public. This pent-up up demand for cars encouraged two entrepreneurs who profited form the manufacture of war goods to get into the booming auto business: Preston Tucker and Henry Kaiser.

George Tator's first full year as a Dodge dealer was 1914. The dealership was initially located in a barn a few miles outside of South Salem, New York. Not only did the barn house the dealership, but also a gas station and the local volunteer fire department's truck. This photo was taken in 1948 when the original 1924 truck was replaced. For 80 years this dealership has remained at the same location and is still run by the Tator family. *C. Tator collection*

facility. V.T. Houser, Sears Vice President in charge of merchandising, indicated that the stores selected to sell the Allstate were already doing a brisk business in tires, batteries, and auto accessories. Houser indicated that the sale of a new car in Sears' stores was the next logical step in Sears' automotive merchandising program. Even though cars were sold out of department stores in the early 1900s, this was the first example of a department store actively merchandising an automobile.

The Allstate was a basic Henry J two-door sedan with Allstate badging on the hood and instrument panel. It was offered in a standard or deluxe model. The customer had a choice of two engines, a four-cylinder L-head rated at 68 or an 80 horsepower L-head six. A three speed manual transmission was standard and an overdrive was optional. Also optional was a heater, turn signals, and

The postwar car-buying boom brought new players into the game. Henry Kaiser made his fortune during the war building ships. He used his capital to finance his new car business. This small Kaiser-Frazer dealership also sold Rototillers. Escondido Historical Society

Tucker, who made his fortune building rotating gun turrets, built the short lived Tucker Torpedo. Tucker's dream ended when he was indicted (and later acquitted) on charges of stock manipulation. Many would-be dealers invested in Tucker's dream, only to lose everything.

After proving he could build Liberty Ships in record time, Henry Kaiser decided to take on the auto industry. He invested $100 million of his own money to start the venture. Along with Joe Frazer, of the former auto maker Graham-Paige, they built the Kaiser-Frazer line of cars and the Henry J. "Back in those days, with the car hungry public, you could sell anything," says Charley DiBari who's father, James DiBari, opened a Kaiser-Frazer dealership in Oakland, California. "The Kaiser was a good car. They were the first ones to start with two-tone paint jobs and fancy interiors, as opposed to everything being gray. They had a lot of good ideas and the product was good. It failed because they didn't have a V8 engine. They couldn't beg, borrow, or steal a V8. That's when the Olds rocket was coming on and everybody was talking horsepower. Kaiser was stuck with the old flat head Continental six." Material shortages also hampered the car's production. Kaiser also joined up with an unusual partner for the sales and distribution of the Henry J.

On November 20, 1951, Sears, Roebuck & Co. announced that it would begin selling a low priced car in 1952. The car–named the "Allstate"–would be built by the Kaiser-Frazer Company at their Willow Run, Michigan,

a radio. All Sears Allstates were equipped with Allstate tires (guaranteed for 18 months), an Allstate battery (guaranteed for 24 months), and Allstate spark plugs.

Sears targeted its stores where the auto accessory trade was highest. It was a regional plan that included selected stores in the South, Southwest, and West. Fayetteville, North Carolina; Little Rock, Arkansas; Orlando, Florida; and Baytown, Texas, were among the 19 Sears retail stores where the Allstate could be purchased and serviced.

The basic Allstate with a four-cylinder engine was priced at an inexpensive $1,395. The Deluxe model with the six-cylinder engine and overdrive would cost a Sears shopper $1,796. Used cars were taken in trade and financing of the Allstate was also done through Sears. Sears policy of "Satisfaction Guaranteed or Your Money

Back" applied to the Allstate. Production of the Henry J ended in 1953, and so too the Allstate.

Montgomery Ward was not to be left out of the car sales game. In the early sixties, some if its stores took on one of the most unique cars ever built–the Amphicar. The German-built Amphicar was brought into the market as a multi-purpose vehicle. Its body was designed like a boat hull, complete with twin screws in the rear. Its market niche targeted those who desired a second car that could be used for running errands. This niche was further narrowed to include the driver who also wanted to drive on the weekend, with the top down, straight into a lake. The Amphicar was sold by anyone who would take on a franchise. This included several dealers who specialized in imports, a few Big Three dealerships, many used cars lots, and even a few small boat dealers

Potts Pontiac typified the many new car dealers that sprang up after the war. Instead of renovating an existing building, this facility was built expressly for the sale and service of automobiles. *Copyright © 1978-1999 GM Corp. Used with permission of GM Media Archives*

got into the act. Between 1961 and 1967, 3,700 Amphicars were imported into the United States and Canada.

In the November, 1956 issue of the trade journal *Automotive News*, Henry Ford II was quoted as saying, "The Edsel ushers in a new era in the automobile industry. It is going to be a proud addition to the Ford family of fine cars. We hope you will share that pride with us as you hear more about this exciting new line of cars." For the booming automotive industry, the news was exciting–Ford was launching an entirely new line of

cars. Current and potential dealers saw dollar signs!

In the Spring of 1957, Ford started to sign up dealers. By June, there were 4,250 individuals who had requested to be considered for one of the auspicious Edsel franchises. It was Ford Motor Company's goal to have 1,200 premier dealerships in place when the Edsel was introduced. J.C. (Larry) Doyle, had been named the Divisions Sales Manager. He was a 40-year veteran of selling Fords and masterminded the dealer recruitment effort. For the new Edsel dealerships, Doyle

CODE OF ETHICS

In 1958, after two years of study, the Automobile Dealers Association of Indiana adopted a Code of Business Standards designed to benefit the public and new car dealers. This voluntary code was designed to instill faith into the much-maligned business of selling cars. The purpose of the code was to promote and maintain honesty and dependability in business operations and to avoid deception and fraud. The code mandated truth and accuracy in advertising for automobiles, parts, and service, stating that the dealer should stand by any guarantee given on a motor vehicle. The code also agreed to maintain fair competition and business ethics between dealers as well as provided a guide to the public to fair and unfair business practices. Ironing out the final wording of the agreement among the dealers took two years, but once ratified, it had to be accepted and believed by the public.

A public relations campaign was put into effect that would use the code to win new friends for Indiana's car dealers. The help of then-governor Harold W. Handley was enlisted to kick off the campaign. From Dealer Association headquarters came special newspaper advertising with certificates for the dealers who sponsored the code. A press conference was held with a prominent list of state, civic, and industrial leaders to announce the dealers' decree.

Only members in good standing of the Automobile Dealer Association of Indiana were eligible to subscribe to the code. Every effort was made to solicit nonmember dealers to join the association. It was agreed that the only way the code would work was if it were supported unanimously. Member dealers were encouraged to meet regularly with the local Better Business Bureau, Chamber of Commerce, and Merchants Associations. At these meetings, dealer representatives would explain the objective of the code. The dealers were encouraged to invite civic leaders and media representatives to these meetings. Local dealers wrote press releases that they distributed to the local media, and in many instances, purchased large newspaper advertisements individually or as a group, touting the benefits of the code. This upbeat campaign made every attempt not to cast aspersions on nonmember dealers. It was felt that with so much positive press, other dealers would join in due course.

The code of conduct approved by the Indiana Dealer Association was exactly what honest and successful dealers had been doing on their own for years. The straightforward dealers of the past and today all have found that doing business honestly and fairly will bring in a steady stream of customers.

approached the top dealer in every town. Applicants were screened by Ford staffers who checked out the candidates by interviewing their bankers, Chambers of Commerce, and other business associates.

By July, 1957, the list of Edsel dealer hopefuls had reached 5,100. When the first list of dealers was released later that month, it read like a Who's Who of the automobile dealer world. Some of the most respected names in the industry had requested a franchise and were among the first to receive one. Most of these new dealers had a well-established relationship with Ford Motor Company as either a Ford, Lincoln, or Mercury dealer. Others on the list were willing to give up their existing franchise to obtain the cherished Edsel charter. At that time, car dealers sold only a single manufacturers product line. Any dealer selling General Motors or Chrysler products had to relinquish those franchises to get the nod from Edsel. "Edsel franchises were very much sought after," says Ken Stevens, who's father obtained an Edsel franchise and would eventually open Cass Edsel in Wyandotte, Michigan. "People were giving up GM franchises. Back then you represented only one dealer, that was your persona–you were known as Mr. Chevrolet or Mr. Oldsmobile." Steven's father had been one of the most successful Packard dealers in the Detroit area when Edsel approached him. "There were very few Edsel franchises given to independents," says Stevens. "Most were given to Ford or Lincoln-Mercury dealers. Edsel was the hot franchise to have in 1958!"

By September, 1957, there were 1,176 Edsel dealers in place, ready to sell cars. Thirty percent of these dealers had other Ford or Lincoln-Mercury franchises. Forty-nine percent of the new Edsel dealers came from the ranks of General Motors, Chrysler or other manufacturers. Former Ford employees accounted for 8 percent, 7 percent were used car dealers, and the final 6 percent were individuals who had never been in the auto business before.

Dealership designs followed the architectural trends of the day. Kidney-shaped swimming pools and coffee tables with their smooth curves were popular in the 1950s. The design of this dealership mirrors that trend with the smooth rounded corners on the large sign and front edge of the roof. The exceptionally large plate glass windows gave passersby a good view of the cars in the showroom. By this time, some of the symbols, such as Chevrolet's bow tie, had become iconic.

The two items that add the most value to an automobile dealership are its longevity and customer relationships. A well-established dealer, like Detroit, Michigan's, Jerry McCarthy Chevrolet, has built solid relationships with customers for decades. These longtime customers return year after year to buy cars, parts, and service. *Copyright © 1978-1999 GM Corp. Used with permission of GM Media Archives*

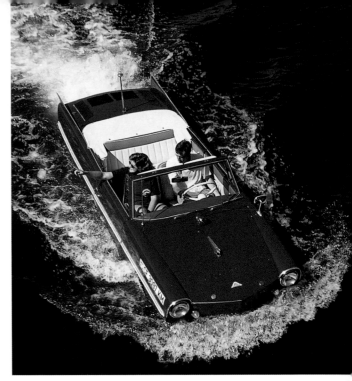

The Amphicar was a unique combination of boat and car. In the mid 1960s, it was sold by department stores, marinas, and established automobile dealers.

Just down the street from Jack Powell's De Soto-Plymouth dealership is Peto Motors, a Lincoln-Mercury dealer. Both dealers would be competing for some of the same customers, because De Soto and Mercury were both selling the same class of car. *Escondido Historical Society*

In 1957, setting up a new Edsel dealership was not an inexpensive proposition. The average Edsel dealer invested between $75,000 and $125,000 to set up shop. It was estimated that $5 million was spent by new Edsel dealers for shop tools and equipment alone.

The new Edsel franchise holders were told they were to operate on a "profit center" concept. The four profit centers were to be new cars, used cars, service, and parts and accessories. Long before the dealers received any cars, they were sent a publication titled, "Your Edsel Marketer," which outlined management, marketing, and merchandising ideas. These new dealers were also sent a copy of "Edsel Dealership and Facilities Guide." This 35-page book detailed how to select and decorate an Edsel dealership facility. Everything was covered in this guide, from counter heights to square footage allotted for restrooms. Edsel left nothing to chance in building product identity and uniformity in their dealership facilities.

Edsel conducted direct training at 12 training centers. In addition, there were 12 mobile training units that were on the road visiting new dealerships. These mobile units were trailers setup as classrooms, towed to the various dealerships by Ford station wagons.

The first meetings for Edsel dealers was held in Dearborn, Michigan, in August of 1957. It was there that the new dealers would get their first glimpse of the new Edsel.

Shortly after, on August 27 and 28, the motoring press would get their first look. Over 250 reporters from across the country attended the two-day event. In Ford's words, they created "a daring challenge" for the journalists. Each of the reporters was invited to drive a new Edsel from the press preview back home and deliver it to his local Edsel dealership. Sixty-five took the challenge, but not all of them arrived home in the Edsel. Several of the new Edsels died on the road and made inauspicious debuts as they arrived at their destination on the hook of a tow-truck. It was only a shadow of things to come.

September 4, 1957, was New Car Introduction Day for Edsel. During the first week, Ford estimated that 2.8 million people visited Edsel showrooms. It was also during that week that the first Edsel was reported stolen. One journalist quipped that the theft of an Edsel demonstrated the public's acceptance of the new model. One week prior to the introduction date, a new Edsel was spotted on a used car lot in Cleveland. The dealer who had sold the car to the used car dealer apologized to his 1,175 fellow Edsel dealers via telegram.

Although the excitement of the new car brought people into the showrooms, they were not driving away in new Edsels. Only 1,566 were sold the first month, far below the projected number of cars to be sold in order for the Edsel to be profitable. Ford did not project Edsel sales to be in black ink the first year, but they did expect a reasonable showing.

One Sunday night in 1957, in order to get the attention of the American public, Ford pre-empted the legendary Ed Sullivan Show to air a television special for the Edsel. Since nearly every TV set in the nation was tuned to the Ed Sullivan Show, Ford expected to capture the entire audience to push the Edsel. The program starred Frank Sinatra and Bing Crosby and was said to have cost Ford an estimated $400,000. This extravaganza did little to stimulate sales.

By November, 1957, the big Edsel hot air balloon was running out of gas and losing altitude fast. Charles Kreisler, a well respected New York auto dealer, closed his Edsel franchise in favor of one for American Motors. Kreisler had given up a profitable Oldsmobile franchise

When Ford announced that an all new car was going to be built and marketed, people clamored to be on the list of prospective dealers. Many individuals were required to relinquish their competing franchises to be able to sell the Edsel. After the Edsel was discontinued in 1960, many franchise owners sued Ford Motor Company to recoup their losses. *From the collections of Ford Motor Company*

On October 1, 1958, the face of car buying was changed forever. From that date forward, a "Monroney label"— better known as a price sticker—would be attached to the window of each new car. The addition of this simple piece of paper to the car window helped restore customer confidence in auto dealers by taking away the "smoke and mirrors" of trying to figure out the actual price of the car.

Senator A. S. Mike Monroney, a Democrat from Oklahoma, was the chairman of the Subcommittee on Automobile Marketing Practices of the Senate Interstate and Foreign Commerce Committee. Senator Monroney's subcommittee spent three years investigating the sales and marketing practices of automobile dealers. The subcommittee's chief witness was John O'Brien, president of the Akron, Ohio, Better Business Bureau. O'Brien testified that one of the reasons that auto sales had declined in 1958 was that consumers were fed up with dealers' "tricks, gimmicks, and somersaults." It was difficult to shop for a car when every dealer offered a different price for the same car. Senator Monroney's report stated, "Alone among commodities on the American market, the automobile purchaser finds himself without that most essential single bit of consumer information—the price of the product." The Senate's interest in automobile marketing practices was not only for the consumer's protection, but because of the large impact the automobile business had on the entire U.S. economy at that time (over $30 billion in 1958).

The "Truth-In-Labeling" law, as it was officially known, required the manufacturer to affix a sticker to the windshield, window, or other "prominent place" on the vehicle.

On this sticker would be listed the suggested retail price of the vehicle, the cost of optional equipment, handling, delivery charges, and federal taxes. The only additional costs that would not appear on the window sticker were local taxes and any dealer-installed accessories. Removal or alteration of the price sticker by the dealer was punishable by up to one year in prison and a $1,000 fine.

The price sticker also eliminated the practice of "packing." Packing was a tactic of inflating the value of the customer's trade-in, which made it appear to the finance company that the person was qualified for a loan on the car they were about to purchase. Unbeknownst to the consumer and to the finance company, the dealer had increased (packed) the price of the new car. Let's assume that a customer brings in a trade that's worth $700 and wants to buy a car that costs $2,700. In 1958, most finance companies required 33 percent down, so this customer falls short at 26 percent. If the dealer inflates the trade-in by $300 to $1,000 and increases the price of the new car by $300 to $3,000—the magical one-third down is reached. What the customer and finance company didn't realize is that the customer just took out a $300 loan on the old car being traded-in. With the packed price, the customer's equity and credit position is distorted. With the new price sticker, the customer could see the true cost of the new car and packing ceased to be a problem.

From a public relations standpoint, the introduction of the price sticker did more to restore public confidence in the car dealers than anything that had happened in the previous ten years. Those who complained the most were those unethical dealers who often fudged the numbers to get the sale.

1959 EDSEL

America's Finest Car in the Low Price Range

	MFR'S. SUGGESTED RETAIL PRICE
RANGER 4 DOOR SEDAN B	2683 50
WHITE SIDEWALL TIRES	35 68
MILE O MATIC DRIVE	189 60
LEVER TEMP HTR & DEFROST	74 45
8 TUBE RADIO	64 95
BACKUP LIGHTS	9 42
FULL WHEEL COVERS	16 60
TWO TONE PAINT	21 55
TRANSPORTATION CHARGES	96 00
TOTAL	3191 75

SOLD TO:

HANCOCK MOTORS INC
SANFORD N C

METHOD OF TRANS.

CONVOY

SHIP TO (IF OTHER THAN ABOVE)

VEHICLE SERIAL NUMBER | ASSEMBLY PLANT

C9UF 729551 LOUISVILLE KY

LABEL IS AFFIXED PURSUANT TO FEDERAL AUTOMOBILE INFORMATION DISCLOSURE ACT. MANUFACTURER'S SUGGESTED RETAIL INCLUDES REIMBURSEMENT FOR FEDERAL EXCISE TAX AND SUGGESTED DEALER PREPARATION AND CONDITIONING CHARGE. ANTI-FREEZE, LICENSE AND TITLE FEES, STATE AND LOCAL TAXES, AND DEALER INSTALLED OPTIONS AND ACCESSORIES.

IMPORTANT!

These quality features included in every Edsel at no extra cost!

- Aluminized muffler
- Self-adjusting brakes for lining wear
- Foam-rubber front seat cushion
- Baked enamel finish
- Guard-Rail Frame with full length, full-strength box-section side rails
- Double-gripping safety door locks
- Recessed-hub safety steering wheel
- Safety tubeless tires and wide-rim design wheels
- Safety glass in every window
- Full-view turn indicators

plus MANY MORE

Ask your salesman about other luxury features Edsel provides as standard equipment in this model.

EDSEL DIVISION
FORD MOTOR COMPANY

The 1958 "Truth-In-Labeling" law gave the consumer a way to compare the prices of similar cars. A window sticker, also known as the "Monroney sticker" for the bill's author, was to be affixed to each new car. Automakers soon realized that this also gave them another place to advertise.

The American car dealership with its neon lights and classic signs has been a part of the American roadside landscape for 100 years. The dealership is a place where automotive dreams are made—and can come true. *Copyright © 1978-1999 GM Corp. Used with permission of GM Media Archives*

to acquire Edsel. By the end of November, 18 other Edsel dealers would quit.

Early in December, 1957, Edsel launched a hard-sell promotion. One and a half million letters were sent out to the owners of other medium-priced cars. The letter invited them to test drive a new Edsel at their local dealership and by doing so, they were promised a scale model. By December, all Edsel dealers were hurting for business. Henry Ford II appeared on a special, closed-circuit television broadcast to let them know "the Edsel is here to stay." Unfortunately, he was wrong.

In November, 1959, Ford issued a press release that stated, "Retail sales have been particularly disappointing and continued production of the Edsel is not justified." Production of the 1960 model totaled only 2,846 units. Ford followed up by offering Edsel owners a $300 certificate to be applied to the price of any other Ford product.

Along with Ford Motor Company, the Edsel dealers took it on the chin. Many had given up lucrative dealerships and had invested their own money, only to lose it all. In 1962, two former Edsel dealers from Iowa sued Ford Motor Company for misrepresenting the car prior to its introduction in 1957. These dealers claimed that Ford positioned the new Edsel as superior to similar cars and that it would be a leader in innovations for comfort and safety. They also claimed that Ford's surveys inaccurately showed that the Sioux Falls area had a customer base for the Edsel. In 1960, a Vermont Edsel dealer sued Ford on the same grounds and was awarded $75,000 on the eve of the trial.

It wasn't until the 1980s that another big new car venture was launched–the DeLorean. Prospective dealers were lining up to invest in a franchise for what was sure to be a winner. They were anxious to sell this new sports car designed and marketed by the man who turned the letters GTO into an American icon. Unfortunately, this dream ended on video tape in a Los Angeles hotel room with a cash and cocaine deal that went sour.

The automotive world owes a great deal to the independent businessmen who, in some cases, risked everything they owned to get into the car business. The early pioneers took an unproven product and sold it to a wary public. At times, these dealers were bullied by the manufacturers and often had to accept inferior products. Many were ordinary men with a dream and a solid work ethic. Others were visionaries who were able to peek into the future and see wide stretches of roads criss-crossing America. On those roads were American families driving to their favorite getaway in a new car. As automakers have come, gone, and merged–the American automobile dealer franchise system has survived and flourished.

In the 1950s and 1960s, brand loyalty restrained a dealer from owning a competing franchise. Today, auto dealers, like San Diego's John Hine, carry Mazda, Pontiac, and Chrysler-Plymouth in the same showroom.

The small local dealer on Main Street has given way to large auto parks, or auto malls, where every business on the street is a car dealership. Competition is keen, because each dealer knows the customer can walk next door and bargain for a similar car.

CHAPTER 2

DEALERSHIP ARCHITECTURE AND LOCATION

FROM STORE FRONT TO AUTO MALL

The earliest automobile dealerships were converted auto repair garages. These garages were outgrowths of bicycle sales and repair shops and blacksmith shops. Bicycle mechanics were the most familiar with the drive mechanisms used on the early cars, which in most cases were converted bicycle hardware. Blacksmith shops either built or repaired wagons and were familiar with chassis and coach construction and repair. The blacksmith shops were well equipped to do heavy repair work and offered a facility that would allow automobiles to drive inside. Parts were often not available and the blacksmith found it easier to fabricate components for the disabled automobile. It was only natural to promote the auto repair business by selling more cars. In many cases, the repair shop acquired a car that the owner no longer wanted. Many of these shops sold the cars and found it to be a lucrative business. More often than not, the repair shop acquired a franchise to sell one or more makes of cars.

In 1912, Casper, Wyoming, was an oil boom town. The population was increasing, and the demand for cars was huge. That year, an oil gusher came in at the Salt Creek field, just north of town. More wells were being drilled, pipelines laid, and refineries built. It was also at this time that Casper received its second rail line. With a solid and wealthy customer base begging for cars and a rail connection ready for delivery, it was only a matter of time before someone would capitalize on the opportunity.

That someone was P. J. O'Connor, who started his empire by building Casper's Coliseum Amusement Hall on the corner of 5th and Wolcott. The Coliseum housed a dance floor, a skating rink, and a bowling alley. It was constructed from lumber purchased from an overstocked railroad project. Even though Casper was booming, it wasn't ready for a large amusement center and within a year, the doors were closed. So in 1913, O'Connor and several investors decided to use the Coliseum building as an automobile repair facility and new car agency. The first cars sold there were Chandlers. Soon, O'Conner received one of the first contracts to sell Dodge cars. Neither manufacturer could supply cars at the rate at which they were being sold. Within a few years, Coliseum was also selling Paige, Hudson, Franklin, Pierce Arrow, Peerless, and Cadillac automobiles and seven makes of trucks. Because of their sales activity, the Coliseum would accept cars from any manufacturer willing to ship them a boxcar full.

Exterior signs are an important part of any dealership property. Certain manufacturer's logos, shapes, colors, and scripts have become instantly recognizable by motorists. At night, this authorized Ford and Mercury dealer's sign is illuminated by neon. *Howard Ande*

In 1917, the rapidly expanding enterprise was incorporated into the Coliseum Garage Company and then into the Coliseum Motor Company. With a substantial group of investors, several other associate dealerships were opened in the area.

The Coliseum Motor Company remained a fixture in Casper through boom and bust cycles of Wyoming's oil and uranium ventures. Soon Dodge became the only product they sold and in 1933 they were named one of the twelve most successful Dodge dealers in the country. In 1956, the original wooden building partially collapsed. In 1957, a new two-story brick building was constructed, which still stands today.

Like Coliseum Motors, much of the early automobile dealership construction was of wood. In the colder northern climates, brick buildings were fashionable. The designs were simple commercial buildings with a large door facing the street, which was used as a vehicle entrance into the rear service area. Space was allotted in the front for offices and for the display of one or more new vehicles.

In urban downtown areas, many dealerships were converted store fronts. A two-story building along Main Street that may have been a furniture showroom could be converted for the display of new cars and servicing in the back. Converting an existing building into a dealership posed some problems, however. For instance, moving cars around inside an existing building with support columns posed some obvious logistical challenges. It wasn't until the early 1920s that purpose-built automobile dealerships began to appear. One of the most beautiful of the early dealerships was the one built by D. E. Stetler in York, Pennsylvania, in 1923.

In 1914, Daniel E. Stetler, who was a butcher in Newberrytown, Pennsylvania, borrowed money from his uncle to get into the new car business selling Dodges. While the car business was getting up to speed, Stetler continued to cut meat. By 1920, Stetler had become a full-time auto dealer and moved his operation into an existing brick structure on Roosevelt Avenue in the much larger city of York, Pennsylvania.

The auto business in York, Pennsylvania, was booming in the early 1920s. Stetler, along with several other dealers and garages, announced plans to build new facilities. Local newspaper articles detailed the plans of York's new automobile dealership buildings. Stetler's Dodge dealership was to be built on South George Street on the former site of the Stark Hotel. Of all the new dealer construction in York, this location was deemed to be the best.

The Coliseum Garage was originally built as an amusement center in Casper, Wyoming, in 1912. In 1913, it was converted to an auto repair facility and new car agency for many brands. This building stood until 1956 when a portion of the building collapsed. The dealership was moved to a new location where it stands today. *R. Robertson collection*

The building Stetler constructed was a showplace in the art deco style. It featured custom tile work and semi-classical detailing above the large showroom windows. In the center of the building was a large entrance that was also used to move cars in and out of the showroom. Specially designed wooden ramps were used to facilitate driving the cars over the curb and steps. The building's pitched roof was concealed by steps that led to a circular pediment. Within that pediment was a stained glass Dodge Brothers insignia with interlocking triangles. At the left side of the front of the building was a narrow vehicle entrance that led to the service department in the rear of the building. This type of vehicle entrance on the main street was typical of urban dealerships of the era, and as the only vehicle access door, cars often jammed South George Street waiting to enter.

The inside of Stetler's Dodge dealership was as dramatic as the outside. The showroom had a 20-foot ceiling.

A mezzanine above the showroom housed the dealership's business offices. This level was accessed from the showroom by a 10-foot-wide, open staircase. The showroom and mezzanine were trimmed in oak and the showroom floor was covered in green tile. On one wall of the showroom was a fireplace. This dealership far exceeded all others of the era for visual impact.

All of the elaborate and expensive design features in Stetler's dealership, such as the high ceilings, the fireplace, the oak paneling, and the detailed art deco exterior design, were usually reserved for upscale dealerships such as Auburn, Lincoln, or Cadillac. To find this level of construction expense in a dealership selling mid-priced cars was extremely rare, except in the heart of a metropolitan area like New York or San Francisco.

Soon after opening his doors, Stetler started to expand. He first purchased some old homes on one side of the building. This space was used to expand the parts

Built in the 1920s, Daniel Stetler's Dodge dealership in York, Pennsylvania, was an upscale design in an Art Deco style. Above the windows is extensive custom tile work and elaborate detail. The circular pediment at the top of the building holds a stained glass Dodge Brothers insignia. The opening to the left is the entrance to the service department. *York Historical Society*

department. Later, more old homes were leveled, providing a rear entrance to the service department.

In 1990, the Stetler family moved the dealership to a new facility. The old neighborhood was starting to decay and George Street had been converted into a one-way thoroughfare, making access for customers difficult. The new facility was built on Roosevelt Avenue, the same street where Stetler first had his dealership in the early 1920s. The stained glass Dodge Brother's insignia that had graced the top of the George Street building was moved along with the dealership and today has a place of honor in the new car showroom.

Through the beginning and mid 1930s, the depression halted the building of most new dealerships. Those that were built, especially those in larger cities, were in art deco themes. In the late 1930s, many people were willing to do their part in the recovery from the depression and spent lavishly for their new dealership buildings. Their hope was that money would beget money.

Economic constraints during the Second World War, however, put all new dealership buildings on hold. With no new cars available to sell, a new facility was out of the question, and many dealerships even converted their space to small-scale war goods production. The stagnation of the auto industry during the war years was echoed in

The Butzer Brothers Ford agency also sold tires. The building is constructed of brick and the upper floor is probably apartments. The sign hanging off the front of the building lists prices for the 1914 Ford touring car and runabout.

Auburn-Cord dealerships were some of the most elegant. While small, this building has outstanding detail in the brick work. The expanse of windows reveals a showroom that extends the full width of the building. *Auburn Cord Duesenberg Museum*

architectural development. No new designs were forthcoming, and the only new buildings being designed and built were commercial buildings for defense production. All of that would change following the war.

The strong demand for cars after the war ultimately stimulated the construction industry. New dealerships were blossoming in every city and town. New purpose-built dealership buildings were in demand. Adapting an existing building for the sale of new cars was not good enough anymore. Within a few years, showrooms would be filled with new modern cars and the dealerships had to have facilities that reflected these designs. By the late 1940s, the manufacturers would be

providing dealers with comprehensive architectural planning guides for automobile dealer properties and facilities. These guidebooks presented current and future dealers with ideas to keep their property and facilities functional and modern well into the future. They presented concepts to help the dealer with the effects of traffic, merchandise, and location, as well as enabled dealers to analyze space requirements and to select features that would yield a greater return on investment, from remodeling or new construction. They were also used as an aid in recognizing sales opportunities through the appropriate use of property design.

The interior of an Auburn dealership was nicely furnished. Everything in this showroom enhances the feeling of elegance and style. The 1932 Auburn 8-100 Cabriolet's wheels are resting on small carpeted risers. *Auburn Cord Duesenberg Museum*

General Motors compiled one of the best of these guides in a hardbound edition, *Planning Automobile Dealer Properties*, published in 1948. General Motors asked their own dealers to name the features they would like in a new dealership building. These dealers were also asked which features they would eliminate in a new facility. General Motors then sponsored an architectural design competition for automobile dealerships. This competition was approved by the American Institute of Architects and the Royal Architectural Institute of Canada, and a blue ribbon jury was assembled. When published in 1948, this guide became an important tool to any franchise holder looking to build a new facility or remodel an existing building.

The new dealership designs of the late 1940s were intended to be merchandise and service oriented and to showcase new cars through a well-organized store front. A store front is one of the dealer's best means of advertising its products and services. The term "store front" includes not only the exterior elevation of the building and property that borders on a street, but also the view that extends into the showroom and to the signs that are placed in the front, side, and rear of the building. Dealers are interested in any elevation feature that will make traffic stop, look,

These two photos are of the same Auburn-Cord-Dusenberg dealership that was located on Wilshire Boulevard in Los Angeles. The photo above was shot in 1932 and the photo on the right was taken in 1937. This building is typical of the Art Deco style prevalent in upscale buildings in metropolitan areas in the early 1930s. One of the elements that characterizes Art Deco is the use of simple, repeating patterns. *Auburn Cord Duesenberg Museum*

In 1936, Lippincott Motors in Grand Rapids, Michigan, sold both Oldsmobiles and GMC trucks. This highly detailed brick building was probably built for a retail business other than cars and then later converted. Another interesting detail is the placement of floodlights on the roof. The lights do not point at the sign, but are at right angles to the building. *Courtesy Oldsmobile History Center*

Edwards Motors was a Kentucky-based Auburn-Cord dealership. The center window on the second floor provides a frame for the car on display. The two other second floor windows are painted over, displaying signs for the service, parts, and used car departments. In keeping with the upscale theme, a canopy is used to cover the pedestrian entrance to the showroom. *Auburn Cord Duesenberg Museum*

and enter the dealership. A well-organized store front is one of the dealer's best advertising mediums, because it is located at the point of sale and presents a three-dimensional color merchandising panorama intended to arouse immediate customer interest.

Dealer interest in the design of a store front is much broader than can be depicted in the views of an architect's drawing. Previously, architectural drawing views were limited to a single point, fixed view. They were also drawn at angles that showed as much of the building as possible, even though a customer on the street might never see that view of the building. The dealer had to be concerned with how the store front was perceived by a motorist driving past the building. Today the problem of a moving perspective has been solved with computer-aided design and simulation that allow the viewer's perspective to move around the building.

In the 1920s and 1930s, dealership interior layouts and exterior elevations were planned separately. Following the war, merchandising demanded that the interiors and exteriors be planned together if they were to be effective. The architects realized that the interior and exterior of a modern dealership were inseparable parts of a single selling unit.

It has always been good architectural practice to plan the functional requirements of an automobile dealership

(or any business) ahead of esthetic requirements. Each individual department must have adequate floor space to function properly. Giving first consideration to functional requirements does not mean that the store front appearance must yield to a set floor plan. These departmental plans often must be modified to achieve a store front design that has unity and a good overall appearance.

Beauty is only one element in dealership store front design. The main objective is to increase the selling efficiency of the dealership, which means developing the store front to convey the message of the institution and each individual department in harmony. Departmental

display signs should be grouped to deliver a more forceful advertising message than they could individually.

Dealership store fronts use some very simple devices to catch the eye of customers: size, contrast, pattern, movement, color, and brightness. The human eye is drawn to and comprehends large objects more quickly than it does small objects. Because automobile dealerships are inherently larger than most other retail businesses, they can take advantage of the advertising potential by using the size of the building. Typically, more height is needed for a service department; and in many cases that vertical size can be used to attract attention at little extra

This Chevrolet showroom is filled with 1929 car and truck models. This dealership was probably located in the downtown area of a medium to large city. The ornate chair and desk seem out of place in such a modest showroom.

This Auburn-Cord building was a purpose-built dealership. Like most other new upscale construction of the era, the design reflects the Art Deco style. The fluted columns are Greco-Roman; they are capped at the top with three additional angular details added on each face. The only break from a pure Art Deco look is the small layer of tile between the columns above the doorway. *Auburn Cord Duesenberg Museum*

cost. The width of the store is not always rigidly defined by the frontage at the building line. The dealership's store front width may be effectively increased by angling showroom windows, recessing doors, or using setbacks. Open store fronts that display the depth of the showroom also have the effect of increased size.

Contrasts that provoke comparisons are another way of gaining attention. These contrasts may be between a store front with its surroundings or between the building's interior and exterior. Along a street where the neighboring stores are single story structures, the contrast of a two-story dealership will stand out. Vertical contrast can also be achieved with sign towers. Conversely, in a section of town with multi-story buildings, a single-level dealership will be in strong contrast.

Contrast provides novelty, but extremes need to be avoided when designing a dealership. Architectural fads based on contrast often lack purpose or functionality and soon lose their appeal and attention value. In a community where a certain style of architecture is current, a new building style would provide contrast, but might also be offensive to the business district. A colonial style dealership in a section of town with predominantly Spanish-style buildings creates an unwanted contrast. Contrast must be apparent, but not to a point of conflict.

A subtle way of providing contrast in a dealership building is with the use of texture, finish, and color.

Rough surfaces contrast with smooth, shiny with matte, and dark against light. Contrast is most effectively used in signage.

Colors and materials may be effectively used in patterns that will attract attention. Dealerships from the 1920s and 1930s were heavily influenced by the Art Deco movement. These Art Deco buildings often relied on intricate details. Art Deco store fronts were designed for traffic that moved by slowly (often foot traffic) where the building's details could be examined. As the speed of traffic increased, these intricate patterns gave way to flowing lines and continuous moldings. In the late 1940s, lines gave way to mass, as the force needed to attract and impress fast-moving vehicular traffic became greater.

The use of mass in forming the predominant pattern of a dealership is expressed in windowless second stories, large solid sign elements, and sign towers. Some of the dealership store front elements are given a three-dimensional appearance with the use of color or by extending exterior walls through to an interior wall. Interiors are also used as dominant elements in many modern dealership designs. Visual fronts accent interiors through the use of large glass areas. Walls and piers become a framework for the windows, rather than as separate elements that attract attention.

In 1957, when Ford Motor Company was getting ready to introduce the Edsel, they assembled a dealer facility guide that was given to all Edsel franchise holders. This

Like the Ford Oval and Chevrolet bow tie, the Pontiac Indian head is one of those highly identifiable automobile logos. This one is outlined in red neon tubes.
Howard Ande

guide detailed the Edsel Division's philosophy on colors and color schemes for dealer facilities. This guide stated, "Color attracts! Color identifies! Color sells! Color can give your dealership the look that spells 'Edsel'—and *sells* Edsel—to everyone who comes within seeing distance."

The distinctive Edsel colors were Edsel High-Light Gray for all exterior building surfaces. This was to be offset with a large Edsel logo of a white "E" within an Edsel Green circle, surrounded by a metallic ring. The color scheme of Edsel Green and Edsel High-Light Gray were also suggested to be used on the inside of all department spaces. The idea was to have the colors of the building be as recognizable as the product logo.

Variations in the shape of the building's construction elements are used to attract attention to the dealer-ship. The front of a dealership that contains a series of windows that are exactly the same size and shape may lack an interesting pattern. Interest in the front of the dealership can be aroused by an off-center entrance that varies in size and angle from the windows. Variations in shape should not obscure the overall theme of the building. Often patterns cause confusion and draw the customer's eye to other elements of the building.

Attention can be drawn to an automobile dealer-ship by using movement. The most common use of movement on dealership store fronts is seen in the use of electric signs. Mechanical devices can rotate the sign or sequentially blink the sign's incandescent lights. In dealerships with large showrooms, cars are often placed on turntables and are left to rotate 24 hours a day.

This Chevrolet dealership showroom is a showcase of Art Deco design. Each of the support columns is intricately decorated with illuminated panels. The walls carry the same theme with horizontal detailing and integrated lights. Each of the new 1938 Chevrolets is displayed on its own individual Persian rug. Leather covered chairs are strategically placed throughout the showroom and elegant flower displays suggest affluence.

Clocks and thermometers are other mechanical devices that have been used on the exterior of dealerships to attract attention.

Often, a small business will use color to distinguish itself from other businesses in the same block. Competition between unrelated stores often produces a palate of contrasting colors resulting in little distinction for any individual store. On streets characterized by buildings in a variety of colors, dealers can attract attention by using one color for the entire front of the building. Different shades of the same color can be used for signs and accents.

Surveys have determined that the brightness of an object is the main factor in attracting attention and arousing interest. The more light that stimulates the eye, the quicker objects are seen. The brightness of a dealership building is usually reserved for displays and signs. The brightness of solid materials is often subdued to direct more attention to vehicle displays and signs.

One of the most important features of a dealership store front is the windows. In older dealerships, the windows were thought of as parts of the wall separating the inside from the outside. The displays behind those windows were designed primarily for pedestrian traffic.

In 1948, General Motors produced a book titled, *Planning Automobile Dealership Properties*. In it were several renderings of suggested dealership facilities and floor plan designs. This particular layout is for a dealership with a gas station.

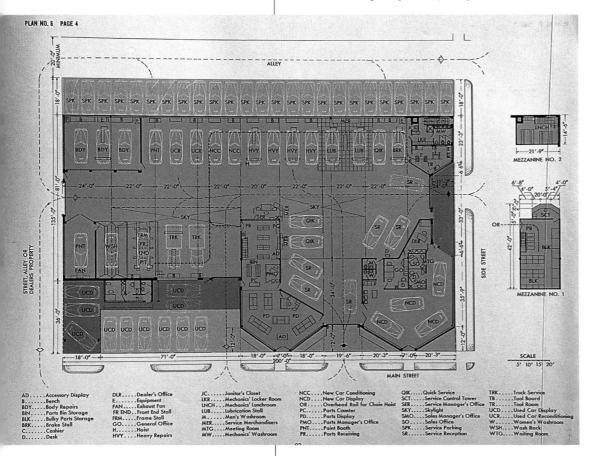

In 1946, Conway Motors also sold Fordson tractors and pumped Shell gasoline. This attractive brick dealership is typical of midwestern construction in the late 1930s. *From the collections of Henry Ford Museum & Greenfield Village and Ford Motor Company*

Dealership design trends in the late 1940s opened the interior to the street. Every attempt was made to make the glass that separated the inside from the outside as inconspicuous as possible. This architectural design concept is known as the "visual front."

In visual front dealerships, the windows are located to create the illusion that there is no glass between the outside and inside by carrying the outside wall materials around to the inside wall and beyond the glass. Large panes of glass supported by small division bars help to foster the visual front concept. In addition, the floor treatment of the showroom may be extended to the exterior of the building which adds to the illusion that there is no visible barrier to the interior of the dealership.

One of the most visible and recognizable parts of any automobile dealership is the sign that identifies the

car line being sold. Whether it's the stylish Ford script, the Chevrolet bow tie, Edsel "E," or the Pontiac Indian head, they are all highly identifiable as to the automotive product being sold or serviced under that sign. An advertising trademark or brand name is the quickest way to acquaint customers with the identity of a business and need to be visible to motorists on all routes that pass the dealership. This visibility is important to an out-of-town visitor who may be having car trouble and is looking for an authorized dealer to take their car for repairs. This brand identity is even used on additional exterior signs that describe the dealership's other services.

Automobile dealership sign location, size, background, message, lettering, color, and lighting are all important. Signs that advertise the product or dealership name should be located so that they are visible to approaching traffic, perhaps by placing the sign at a 90-degree angle to street traffic and overhanging the sign from the building where code permits. Signs that are located at right angles to traffic produce the most advertising value at a lower cost. Most of these dealer signs face in two directions, getting the message out to traffic flowing in both directions on the street.

The size of a dealership sign is dependent on local building codes. Obviously, the larger, the better. Ideally, it should be large enough to be seen distinctly from the most distant point at which the sign becomes visible. Keeping the sign tastefully in proportion to the overall size of the building is also important. The size of a dealership sign is also influenced by its shape. A sign that is in the shape of a recognizable automobile trademark is distinguishable from a distance. As the viewer draws closer, the lettering on the sign will become legible. The purpose of a sign on an automobile dealership is to exclaim, not explain. The fewer the words, the more quickly it can be read.

The background on a dealership sign is as important as the white space around a print ad. Visually, it's the first part of a sign to catch the viewer's eye, because it's larger than the lettering upon it. These large plain backgrounds hold interest because they are restful for the eye; they eliminate distracting detail and provide contrast for the sign's lettering. Dealerships with windowless second and third stories provide an excellent plain background for drawing attention to a sign.

The lettering on a dealership sign is designed to be read quickly and easily by passing traffic. The style of the font must be simple and any ornamentation that interferes with the lettering must be deleted. The style of font must be in harmony with the building's architectural style.

Two-dimensional letters are most commonly used on smaller signs that designate dealership departments. Often these signs are lit with spotlights. The larger product or firm name signs use three-dimensional letters, which are more interesting than the flat signs. Three-dimensional signs often use back lighting or edge lighting to gain attention.

Lighting a car dealership's sign extends advertising all night long, especially where a dealership is located on or near a regularly traveled highway. The visibility of the sign depends on the amount of competing illumination along the street. The background of the building also affects the illumination of the sign.

The most common ways of lighting a dealership sign are with exposed lamps, enclosed lamps, floodlights, and silhouette lighting. Exposed lamps are the most common; this includes neon filled tubes and incandescent bulbs. Dealer signs outlined with colorful

neon lights are especially attractive. Patterns of incandescent bulbs can also be used to artfully illuminate a dealer's sign. Many signs also use sequencing units to illuminate incandescent light in a pattern. Because of the intensity of the lights, signs with exposed lights are most effective when viewed from longer distances.

An enclosed lamp sign is one where a box-like enclosure is formed of solid materials with letters cut from translucent material. This type of sign often features opaque letters on a translucent background. This style of sign is lower in brightness than one with exposed lamps. It is attractive and easy on the eyes at close range.

Floodlights are used to illuminate both the lettering and background of signs. This type of lighting is done with fixtures mounted on the roof or cornices of the building, which is effective because of the large amount of illumination beamed by the floodlights. If designed and installed properly, it holds interest because no direct glare reaches the viewer's eye. Improperly installed, floodlights can be a traffic hazard, directing light into the eyes of driver on the street.

Silhouette and shadow box lighting are also effective methods of lighting a dealership sign. Silhouette lighting is accomplished by backlighting opaque sign letters, or illuminating the background behind the letters. Shadow box lighting consists of freestanding letters arranged along the roof or cornice of the front of the dealership. These letters are illuminated from behind. Both of these forms of sign illumination are low in brightness, easy on the eyes, and tend to hold the viewer's interest.

This building was originally designed as a dealership—an elegant and expensive Chevrolet dealership. The showroom suggests a modern/international style, reminiscent of the construction that was going on in Europe at that time. This style is characterized by strong modern lines, openness, with a few large columns. A sweeping staircase ascends to the offices above. While the exact location of this dealership is unknown, dealerships with this quality of construction and level of elegance were nearly always located in the heart of a large metropolitan area.

This Buick showroom, loaded with 1940 models, was typical of a dealership in a large metropolitan area such as New York or San Francisco. The high ceilings give an air of elegance to the upscale Buicks. Dark Persian rugs alongside each car contrast with the light tile floor. Displayed in the front of the showroom is a complete Buick chassis with an engine. The delicious atmosphere of this showroom invites the customer to buy.

Earl Stoyer Oldsmobile-Cadillac-La Salle has a stock of new 1942 Oldsmobiles in the corner showroom. Behind the showroom, extending the length of the building, is the service department. This building is a straightforward industrial/commercial structure of the late 1930s. It's constructed simply of poured concrete and nicely finished in brick. The gas pumps lined up along the curb indicate that this building may have originally been a garage.

The manufacturer does national advertising in all types of media; but, when it comes down to the local level, each dealership must sell itself. Over the years, local print ads tended to look the same. The one place a dealer could distinguish itself from the others was with its appearance. Often a customer's interest is drawn to an intriguing showroom display. The dealer's everyday showroom display is a mirror of the dealer's philosophy. It need not be elaborate or spectacular. In fact, a simple display will often make a more powerful statement to the potential customer. If they like what they see, customers are more likely to stop in. Large window banners often obscure the cars. A showroom banner proclaiming "We Can Beat Anybody's Deal" might give the potential customer the impression that this dealer is more likely to finagle a deal, rather than sell a car with service and integrity.

The look of a dealership's showroom has a great deal of sales power. An all-glass design provides maximum visual impact and reflects an aggressive business personality that instills confidence in the customer. This type of design beckons the buyer to stop, look, and enter. A drab, outmoded showroom has a negative impact that urges customers to look elsewhere. Dealers who have modernized their facilities see increases in floor traffic and subsequent business.

One-car showrooms were the norm for small town dealers who often converted an existing building to suit their needs. Behind this 1946 Ford sedan is the salesman's desk. In the background are the business offices. *From the collections of Henry Ford Museum & Greenfield Village and Ford Motor Company*

This small Chevrolet-Oldsmobile dealership has room for only three cars in the showroom. The difference in the type of brick indicates that the showroom was probably added to the existing building in the rear. The massive structure on the roof will likely support another dealer sign or billboard space.

The building for this Studebaker dealership probably started life as a garage and was converted some time after. Its construction is of cinder block. The steps at the top of the building front hide the roof's pitch. The ornate detailing above the center service door was probably added when the Studebaker sign was installed. A new 1951 Studebaker sits in the small showroom to the right and out front is a Hi-Arc gas pump.

A large glass front showroom is a silent salesman that confirms in the potential customer's mind that this dealer sells not only cars, but service, cleanliness, dignity, and prestige. A glass showroom creates a showcase for shiny new cars, helping potential customers define their buying preferences.

New Car Showroom

Before the advent of large auto malls, the automobile dealership was one of many businesses along America's Main Street. It had to compete with department and furniture stores for the attention of shoppers. In

fact, many dealerships in the 1920s and 1930s resembled their home furnishing counterparts. Automobile showrooms faced the street with large plate glass windows and awnings above. Behind those windows was the product—the new car. But, because of the relative size of the car in relation to the dealer's windows, it could not be distinguished as readily as a mannequin in a department store window. In the 1940s dealers learned that to sell cars they had to merchandise better through the layout of the dealership and especially the showroom, which needed to be better planned in order to encourage car sales.

The new car showroom is where dreams come true, the place where the customer has the chance to thoroughly inspect the new models and begin to formulate a plan to own one. A well-planned showroom enhances sales by guiding customers through a wonderland of shiny new cars, stimulating the customer's desire to buy, where the alluring new car smell intoxicates the buyer. The feel of the interior's supple material and the brilliance of the paint become an opiate to the customer. Here, it's okay, and even encouraged, to open the hood and check out the engine. No one has ever been stopped from sliding behind the wheel of a new car in a showroom. This singular experience can be one of the most effective deal closers, as the customer imagines himself or herself driving home in a new car. Sitting behind the wheel of that new car, the customer forgets about payments and just fantasizes about owning a new car—this new car.

Small towns only required small dealership facilities. Quite often they were dual purpose like this Pontiac-John Deere dealership. The rounded corners and horizontal lines of the brickwork indicate that this small, but attractive, building was constructed in the early 1950s.
Copyright © 1978-1999 GM Corp. Used with permission of GM Media Archives

Even though it only occupies 4 to 11 percent of the total dealership floor space, the new car showroom is the most important part of any dealership. It needs to be the main attraction that stimulates customer interest. From the street, it must stand out above all other store window displays. The showroom should have a relaxed atmosphere. It must be psychologically attractive and physically comfortable. The surroundings should invite customers to enter and look around, as well as complement the new car's appearance without competing for the customer's interest. The showroom should provide favorable conditions for the customer to examine the car's overall appearance and allow the features and details to be inspected. To inspect a car properly, the manufacturers recommend at least 3 feet of space in front of the car, 4 feet in the rear, and 6 feet on each side, or at least 450 square feet of space allotted to each car in the showroom. This space enables the prospect to comfortably walk around the car and open the hood, doors, and trunk. The new car showroom is a place where buying decisions can be made quickly and with confidence.

In the 1940s and 1950s, a dealer designed a new car showroom that could be seen from the outside by the largest volume of vehicle and pedestrian traffic for the longest time. Back then, traffic was the most valuable asset of any retail business. The new car showroom was the mechanism that turned street traffic into floor traffic, and then into customers.

The dealer had to analyze the traffic passing by the dealership's showroom and be able to define why, where, and when traffic passed. The showroom needed to be located and arranged to take advantage of those passing. The most likely new customer passing by was any current car owner. This person had already bought into the dream of car ownership and would be more likely to purchase another car than would a pedestrian or mass transit user. With only seconds of exposure, the dealership showroom must convey to that viewer the product and an image of the business.

The location of the building and the style of architecture determine the showroom's location. A corner location was always best. A showroom located on the corner of a major intersection was even better. It gave the dealer maximum visibility to the largest volume of cross traffic. While waiting for a traffic light to change,

In the late 1940s, Emmert Chevrolet was located on the corner of Grand River and Evergreen Road in Detroit. The neon sign, visible to traffic on Grand River, includes a clock. Above the building, facing the corner traffic, is a large billboard advertising GMAC financing. *Copyright © 1978-1999 GM Corp. Used with permission of GM Media Archives*

Jim Adam's Hi-Speed gas station also sold and serviced Oldsmobiles. It appears as though the gas franchise was in place long before the Olds franchise was acquired. The small showroom to the left, which contains a GMC truck, was added to the original service station building. *Copyright © 1978-1999 GM Corp. Used with permission of GM Media Archives*

When opening a new business, it's a good rule not to stray too far from the architectural style already in place. This New Mexico Ford dealer built an attractive dealership building using stucco and opaque glass blocks. The recessed areas on the front of the building give it a three-dimensional effect that is pleasing and eye catching. The service entrance door is marked with a large neon-outlined arrow. *From the collections of Henry Ford Museum & Greenfield Village and Ford Motor Company*

In the late 1940s, many new dealership facilities were built. These purpose-built buildings emphasized an expansive showroom, like this one, that has three of its sides glassed-in. Unfortunately Chris Volz, the owner of this Cadillac dealership, forgot one of the basic tenets of showroom display—let the passing traffic see the cars in the showroom.
Copyright © 1978-1999 GM Corp. Used with permission of GM Media Archives

the motorist had a lot of time to dream about the shiny new sport coupe in the showroom.

That showroom display was used for two distinct functions, advertising and merchandising. The new car surrounded by the showroom windows was like a three-dimensional sign to attract attention. A single car used for advertising would often be placed on a raised platform. For dealerships with small showrooms, advertising was the main function of their showroom car. Larger dealerships with larger showrooms could place several new cars in the showroom to both advertise and merchandise the cars. Merchandising lets the customers

see, touch, and smell the new product in the showroom. For dealerships with only a one-car showroom, the merchandising took place on a new car lot or in another part of the dealership building.

To adequately display the cars in the showroom, large windows are needed. The best viewing angle is one that is perpendicular to the plane of the glass. Under certain conditions this position can also create a reflection that veils the view of the cars inside. One trick to reduce the glare was to splay the top of the glass outward. Windows tilted away from the sky create unnatural reflections that can distract attention away from the cars in the showroom. Showroom windows should have a vertical height of at least 10 feet, but 12 feet high is best. The bulkhead at the base of the window must be

Mathews Cadillac in Dearborn, Michigan, used two effective styles of signs. On the side of the dealership, a white billboard-size sign denoting "Used Cars," the Mathews name, and a Cadillac emblem, was painted on the natural brick. Above the showroom is a colorful neon sign that has the Mathews name in block letters and the Cadillac name in script. Also included is a small Cadillac emblem above a "V."
Copyright © 1978-1999 GM Corp. Used with permission of GM Media Archives

60

Jensen's Pontiac in Fairview, Oklahoma, has made the most of an older, smaller building by tastefully adding a colorful neon sign in an Art Deco style. Even the entrance has received the retro treatment with stainless steel trim. *Howard Ande*

An impressive showroom is hidden behind the signs, letting everyone know that the new 1967 Buicks are in. High ceilings and large plate glass windows give the showroom a feeling of spaciousness. The mezzanine above is wood paneled and the railing has an interesting design. Most impressive of all is the stone wall to the right.

low enough so as not to block the view of the lower half of the car. Even the placement of the pedestrian door must be such that it does not interfere with the view of the cars in the showroom. The goal of any showroom is to have the fewest number of barriers blocking the potential customer's view of the cars.

Interior colors for an automobile showroom should be selected with caution. Neutral colors are favored because they are easier on the eyes, reflect the most color from any interior lighting, and don't detract from or clash with the cars on display. The old interior designer's

trick of covering one wall with mirrors is an effective way of making a small showroom seem larger. The cars on display in the showroom are typically light in color. Because of the limited amount of natural light available, even with the largest of windows, the showroom must have a sufficient amount of artificial light. Multiple light sources enhance the look of a car and, even on the brightest days, most of the showroom lights will be fully illuminated. After the sun has set, the only light available in the showroom is from artificial sources. It is extremely important that these lights evenly illuminate

This Ford dealership is constructed with cement block painted white with blue accents. The large "Ford" sign to the left is not the standard Ford Motor Company script. The sign to the far right carries the correct Ford script and the small block letters above give the dealership name. *Escondido Historical Society*

the cars on display. Each artificial light source produces a slightly different color of light in relation to sunlight. The colors selected for the cars on display must be compatible with the artificial light source to give the customer a true rendition of the car's color. The best artificial light source is one that accurately reproduces the white light of the sun.

Today, the U.S. car dealers are moving off Main Street. Within most large cities, large multi-square acre tracts of land are devoted only to car dealerships. Several dealerships can be visited within a matter of minutes in these malls. Because brand loyalty is no longer important to the average consumer, they can compare various models and make their buying decision quickly.

The U.S. car dealership has evolved from sheds and small stores to moderate-sized purpose-built facilities to multi-thousand square foot mega-dealers in vast auto malls. Along the way, dealers learned how to merchandise the cars and their business. In the late 1940s, the dealerships took on a look and style all their own. These custom-designed facilities showed off Detroit's newest designs to a car-hungry public. Surrounded by glass in smartly styled showrooms, the new car was king.

This Ford dealership building is sided with sheet-metal panels. The large showroom is bounded on the far side and rear by the service department and in the foreground by the used car lot.

CHAPTER 3

PROMOTIONS

PUTTING THE *SHOW* IN SHOWROOM

Part of the tradition of selling cars has been the celebration and razzle dazzle that dealers have always used to get the attention of the potential buyer—all done to make a name that sticks in the mind of the buyer when the search for a new car begins. Promotions used by dealers are as old as the traveling salesman who sold pots, pans, and elixirs out of a wagon. The idea is to bring a product to the buying public, with a dash of showmanship.

As with any product, the manufacturer must convince the potential customer of the need for the product, which is true of coffee makers, VCRs, and, of course, automobiles. At the turn of the century, few developed roads existed and the perceived need for cars wasn't there. At that time, the automakers had to not only convince the general public that they needed cars, but they also had to convince potential dealers of the market for cars and that they should sell them.

New Car Introduction

New model introduction from 1946 through the early 1970s has often been compared to the World Series of the automobile year. It was an annual event where fans flocked to the showrooms to critique, sigh, and even buy the latest factory creation. Across the nation, hundreds, and in some cases, thousands of people headed to each showroom out of natural curiosity. It was the best time for dealers to take advantage of the free publicity the new car excitement generated. With each person who crossed the dealer's threshold, the potential for sales increased. Many people who came out for new car introduction were there to buy whatever was the latest and greatest. They wanted to be the first one on their block to own a new model. Others came out because their old car had worn out and it was time for a new car.

For the week prior to the new car introduction, the new models arriving at the dealership were shrouded in secrecy. They were hidden in the dark recesses of the dealership far away from the view of onlookers. If not locked away in a secure building, they would be covered with sheets to protect them from prying eyes. Some smaller dealers stored the new models in the personal garages of friends and relatives. Prior to moving the new models into the showroom, the dealership windows would be either painted with whitewash or covered with butcher paper. One or two small openings would be made at strategic locations to give anxious eyes a partial view of one of the new models. Also in the windows would be signs hyping the new models and the date of the new car introduction night. "Announcement day was a very big thing," says Charlie DiBari, whose father, James DiBari, owned Melrose DeSoto/Plymouth, in Oakland, California, in the 1950s. "People would wait with baited breath until it was New Car Announcement Day—it was a big affair. The showrooms would be jammed with people for a few days. A lot of orders would be taken, the whole buying schematic was different than it is right now. Back in those days, there was tremendous brand loyalty. The guy who bought Chryslers—that's all he bought for his life. He didn't go switching around." DiBari's father also generated more excitement than the average dealer by bringing in a local marching band for his new car introduction extravaganzas.

The flashiest of the new models would be displayed inside the showroom at new car introduction. Convertibles and hardtops in the brightest colors would be spit-shined to perfection. Often the service department was where the less flashy four-door sedans and station wagons were held in reserve. Large banners touting the new models were strung up in the showroom and service department. Flags, signs, balloons, and pennants were all part of the dealership's decorations. Out front, large 800-million candlepower carbon-arc searchlights that years earlier scanned the skies for enemy planes were now used to alert people that something special was happening in their neighborhood.

The salespeople were easy to spot. They were the hyper ones who had obviously had too much coffee in preparation for the big night. They all wore their biggest smiles and often a button or hat denoting the latest factory slogan for that year. The hot-shot salespeople saw this as a special night and made the best of the opportunity to work the room, always keeping an eye open for former customers.

Each year, when the new models are released, the manufacturer creates a sales theme. Chevy's theme in 1963 was "Show Time." Also during the 1960s, each manufacturer released several brand new or completely restyled cars. In 1963 Chevrolet introduced the Corvette Stingray. By placing the white convertible in the front of this showroom, it was sure to be seen and attract customers.
Copyright © 1978-1999 GM Corp. Used with permission of GM Media Archives

Patriotic themes have long been favorites for dealership promotions. This Auburn dealership, photographed in 1907, was draped in red, white, and blue bunting. *Auburn Cord Duesenberg Museum*

Each dealer needed to capitalize on this once-a-year opportunity when the showroom was filled with an enthusiastic flood of humanity. Dealers who failed to take advantage of this occasion would feel the effects all year. Enterprising dealers maximized the advantages of the event and turned the new car introduction into a party where refreshments were served, adding an air of conviviality to the event. Tables full of coffee and soft drinks would be spread out for the customers to enjoy while looking at the new models. The office employees were conscripted to brew plenty of hot coffee and replenish trays of donuts and cake. The paper cups and plates were printed with that year's catchy slogan to remind the customers why they were there. A little something to eat or drink would put customers at ease and often prolong their time in the showroom, giving salespeople more time to mingle, answer questions, and explain the features of the newest models.

To keep the cheerful carnival atmosphere going, enterprising dealers would often raffle door prizes. The customer would fill out an entry blank in the showroom and toss it into a box. At designated times, a dealer official would draw a name. The winner would get a certificate for a free oil change, an accessory mirror, or a set of floor mats. The completed entry blanks were kept on file as a prospect list. By spacing out the times of the drawings, the customers would remain in the showroom for an extended period of time, providing the sales staff even more time to make contact with potential customers and giving customers more time to look at the new models. The prizes that were awarded were all designed to get the potential customer back into the dealership at a later date. A certificate for an oil change would bring the customer back into the dealer's service department. While waiting for that service, the customer would spend more time looking at the new models. A certificate for an accessory required a trip to the parts counter, entailing a walk through the new car showroom. These small investments by the dealers often reaped big rewards throughout the year.

New car introduction took place over two or three days. The first day was often by invitation only. These special first nights would be reserved for local business owners who had an ongoing relationship with that dealership as either a fleet customer or as a local vendor that provided an automotive-related service. In the past, at these typically all-male special business showings, the refreshments had a bigger kick than coffee, and cigars were freely passed out to celebrate the new models. Some dealers reserved the first night showing for former customers only. These customers had already proved their loyalty to the dealership and to the brand. Inviting them in for a first look at the new models gave them the feeling that they were important customers, and in fact they were. Many former customers traded every year and would buy a car on the spot. There's nothing like the enthusiasm generated at new car introduction when a SOLD sign is place on the windshield of a showroom model. The salesman who sold the car would make sure everyone in the showroom knew it was sold by announcing loudly to a co-worker, "Lock up the red hardtop—it's just been *sold*." This kind of proclamation confirmed to potential customers that the new models were hot and going fast. If the new car showing was spread out over several days, the cars that were sold from the showroom floor on the first day would stay on the floor for at least a week.

These events offered plenty of souvenirs to take home as well. Customers leaving the showroom without a sales contract for a new car had at least one or two new car brochures in hand. They also had a business card from one of the sales staff and at least one of that year's give-aways. Yardsticks were one of the most inexpensive souvenirs and were usually marked with some kind of slogan about how the new cars "measured up" to the competition. Another common give-away was the key chain featuring the dealer's name, phone number, and address clearly printed on it.

Planning new car introductions began weeks prior to the event. Small towns used TV and radio to let everyone know about the introduction date. Some dealers even had handbills distributed door-to-door. In larger markets where television and radio were too expensive, large print ads would be run in the local newspaper. As the date drew closer, the individual salesmen would look through their list of customers and start sending letters or postcards.

In the late 1950s and early 1960s, Jim Wangers was an account executive who worked for MacManus, John & Adams, Pontiac's advertising agency. At new car introduction, he and members of his staff took the role of the fly on the wall at new car introduction. "We always went to the new car introduction at the dealers," says Wangers. "Not only us, but the factory people too. It used to be a common thing. We'd get together on introduction night and swing through seven or eight dealerships in and around Detroit. We'd have a pretty good read on what the reaction to a new car was."

As big a deal as new car introduction seemed to be, some dealers found it almost an inconvenience. One owner, whose dealership was in a bad area of a large city, had a difficult time drawing people to the showroom at

night, even at new car introduction. The owner knew their factory representatives expected them to throw a big new car introduction gala. They went through the routine of renting search lights and decorating the showroom. But because they knew they traditionally never had many people come to these events, the owner asked all of the office, parts department, and service department employees to come back, with their spouses or a friend, on the night the factory representative was going to attend. "We always had at least 160 people there on the night the factory reps showed up. The place was packed and the music was playing—we set it up every year. The bottom line was sales. Get the sales out!" This particular dealership always had outstanding sales and the factory never caught on to their new car introduction chicanery. This dealer even sold new cars prior to the introduction date, something frowned upon by the manufacturer. His feeling was that a sale is a sale, so why would he want to disappoint a customer by making him wait?

The excitement of new car introduction began to fade in the 1970s when the phrases "energy crisis" and "sticker shock" became part of our lexicon. Another major factor in the demise of the new car introduction hoopla was the influx of imports. The release dates of new import models didn't conform to the American tradition of new car introduction in the fall of the year. They introduced their cars when they were ready. As the

Big promotions bring in big crowds. This Auburn dealership is filled with customers looking at several 1932 models that have been reduced in price. The sign on the window of the Cabriolet in the foreground has the price marked down from $1,598 to $1,085. The hand-painted signs on the pillars advertise mileage and performance figures of various Auburn models.
Auburn Cord Duesenberg Museum

During the Depression, everyone had a hard time selling cars. Expensive luxury cars, like the Auburns pictured here, carried the costly burden of daily operation and maintenance. The signs painted in the window advertise this dealership's low prices and extended payment plan.
Auburn Cord Duesenberg Museum

import segment grew and became more important in the marketplace, domestic manufacturers were forced to react and follow suit.

One of the last big new car introductions was for the 1980 Chevrolet Citation. Chevrolet was releasing it in the spring of 1979, and they did a huge blitz for its introduction. At that time, Joe Veraldi was a salesman at Bell Chevrolet in Tujunga, California. "They rented tuxedos for all the salesmen, had the showroom decorated, searchlights were scanning the sky—it was like a

big Hollywood movie premiere." The dealership opened the doors at 6 P.M., but all the new Citations in the showroom were covered, heightening the sense of anticipation and drama. At 7 P.M. sharp, the owner of the dealership made a short presentation and then uncovered the cars with a flourish. "We only had 12 Citations in the inventory and we sold them all that night," says Veraldi. It was a big deal because Bell Chevrolet was a small dealership that, on average, moved only 12 cars a week. "I happened to sell the very first one that was located right in the middle of the showroom," says Veraldi. "I even remember the guy's name, like it was yesterday—Joe Hamel. And the reason I remember it so well was because the very next day he brought the car back for service—that Citation was a pile of crap. He drove my demo car more in the next six months than he did his own new car." Despite the unfortunate service setbacks for this particular model, the hoopla surrounding new car introduction was successful in attracting the early-adapters—those who wanted to be first to own a new model. "I was sorry to see those new car intros go away," says Veraldi.

Today, new cars are introduced at major auto shows. The public's appetite for spectacular events has moved the public from the local showroom to the convention hall. People are no longer satisfied with free cookies and coffee at a local dealership's new car introduction. In the 1950s and 1960s, new car introduction was a much more important part of the American automotive buying habit. Today, it's a thing of the past.

This Auburn dealership invented an unusual way to promote the value of this 1932, 8-100 sedan by comparing its price per pound to that of other commodities. Even more interesting is the airplane on display in the background. At the time, the Cord Corporation empire owned Stinson, a manufacturer of aircraft.. *Auburn Cord Duesenberg Museum*

Street Sales, Tent Sales, and Other Promotions

Often a local Dealer's Association would stage its own special event. In the summer of 1962, the local automotive dealers association held a street sale in the downtown section of Elmhurst, Illinois. Prior to the sale, large advertisements were placed in local newspapers to promote the event. On the day of the sale, the city's main street was lined on each side with shiny new cars from each dealership. A clown roved the entire length of the street giving out balloons to the children. This family event attracted a large crowd that was able to see all the new cars in one outdoor location. The festivities were covered by the local press and the following day, many photos were printed of the celebration and autos displayed. This type of event cost the dealers little to put on, but it created neighborhood goodwill, some positive press, and a few extra car sales.

The concept of a large, multi-dealer show can also work on a smaller scale. Individual dealers simply take the initiative to have their own special event. It may be a day when the newest models are parked in and around the showroom decorated with balloons and flags denoting the anniversary of the business or other special promotion.

Many auto dealer promotions are tied into a special holiday, like Valentine's Day. A Valentine's Day promotion includes decorations of large red hearts adorning the showroom and cars. Vases of red roses might be placed on tables within the dealership, adding a touch of romance to this annual event. Some dealerships order a bright red convertible to be placed in the middle of the showroom. And of course, roses are given to each female customer who enters the showroom.

Other holidays that serve as a platform for special promotions include the Fourth of July, President's Day, and Memorial Day. For these holidays, the red, white, and blue theme is featured. U.S. flags are patriotically displayed on the cars and around the showroom. The sales staff often wear red, white, and blue striped vests to celebrate the day.

The Indianapolis 500 car race has been a Memorial Day classic for decades. Each year, a new production car is selected as the official pace car. The dealerships selling that model always have a special Indy 500 celebration with cars on display similar to the car pacing the race. A vintage racing car is often on display, too. Impressing potential customers with civic and national pride is never bad for business.

New car introduction was always one of the most exciting times at an automobile dealership. The allure of the new cars drew people into the showroom to see the new models. Many sales were made during new car introduction by those customers who had to be the first on their block to own one of the new models.
Courtesy Oldsmobile History Center

Free auto safety checks were once a great way to show the community that the dealer was civic and safety minded. Ads placed by the dealer in the local newspaper would announce the date, time, and location. Large signs would also be placed along the street to attract drive-by motorists. For these events, a team of the dealer's best mechanics dressed in white coveralls or shop coats would be stationed at the front of the dealership. The dealer's sales staff and service managers would supervise the cars in line. A form would be given to each motorist on which they filled in their name and address. These forms were then added to the dealer's mailing list. The mechanics would swarm over the car checking the lights, brakes, shocks, cooling system, and general condition of the car.

While this safety check was going on, the motorist was directed into the showroom for some refreshments. The refreshments would always be placed at the rear of the showroom so the motorist would have to walk past the shiny new cars. If a problem with the car was discovered, one of the mechanics would mark it on the inspection sheet. This sheet would be given to the motorist by a service writer. It would be that person's job to encourage the motorist to return to the dealership's service department for the needed repairs. Often

the service department would be running a special on oil changes or lube jobs and the motorist would be informed of the dates and prices for these services.

Another way to attract customers to a dealership was to display a fire truck or police patrol car on the lot. Children were fascinated by the equipment and begged their parents to stop so they could look. The local police, fire department, or Red Cross would make presentations on safety. Balloons were available for the children and refreshments for all. These kinds of events showed the dealership's civic concern.

Over the years, dealer promotions have become more and more creative. One of the most inventive promotions was created by Detroit-area Ford dealer Floyd Rice. He came up with an idea that garnered him a list of 6,000 fresh prospects. He did it with a tie-in to a local drive-in theater. In the mid 1950s, drive-in movies were a favorite form of entertainment, a place where you could see a movie in the comfort of your own car. Mr. Rice's idea was to combine the two by awarding a free car to one lucky individual. For eight weeks in the summer of 1955, Floyd Rice Ford distributed free tickets to Oak Park, Michigan's West Side Drive-In theater. Each ticket was good for free admission for the car and driver. On each ticket, the motorist had to fill in his name, address, make, and year of car currently owned, and if he was interested in buying a new car. On a platform in front of the drive-in was a fully reconditioned, used 1951 Ford sedan that one lucky moviegoer would win.

During the eight weeks of the promotion, the drive-in saw attendance more than double. Throughout the duration of the contest, all types of media, including television, were used to promote the contest. At the end of the contest, public interest was at a peak and the awarding of the car culminated in a civic event. The mayor of the city of Oak Park was in attendance along with the current Mrs. Michigan and Ford dealer, Floyd Rice. Following the presentation of the sedan, additional consolation prizes of televisions were awarded.

Rice's promotion was a winner for everyone. Theater attendance increased and the dealership received a list of 6,000 new names, of which 400 were interested in buying new cars.

Another inventive promotion was offered to the citizens of Baltimore, Maryland, in the spring of 1916. When they opened their morning paper, they saw a large advertisement stating, "Automobile With Every Home." The homes, on the 1600 block of Poplar Grove, were two-story, porch-front row houses that included a garage. The garage was advertised as being fireproof and substantially built of metal with a cement floor. The advertisement didn't mention the make or

In the fall of 1940 the economy was strong and interest in the new 1941 models was high. New car introduction at this Chevrolet dealer brought out a throng of curious customers who inspected every inch of this coupe. *Detroit Public Library, The National Automotive History Collection*

model of car that would fill the garage, but it featured a photo of a five-passenger touring car.

In 1924 a similar promotion appeared in another Maryland housing development called Garrett Park. Three styles of houses were offered starting at $4,950. For an additional $150, the new home buyer could add a garage. Add another $708 or $820 (depending on the model) and a new Chevrolet could be parked in that garage. About 40 of these homes were built and they eventually became known as the "Chevy houses."

The "buy-a-house-get-a-car" promotion once again surfaced in 1981 when General Motors Estate Group offered a free car to anyone who bought one of any 100 Detroit-area homes previously owned by recently transferred GM employees. This program was also offered in New York late in 1981. The more upscale the home, the more upscale the car. Those not wanting a new car with their house were offered a price reduction in the amount of the car's sticker price.

In 1959, John Sheehan, president and general manager of Sheehan Buick in Miami, Flordia, was preparing for a two-week vacation. At that time, Sheehan Buick was one of the largest Buick dealers in the South. Sheehan did not want sales to dip in his absence, so he created a two-week sales promotion to foster enthusiasm and increase sales. His theme and selection as a personal replacement ended up being one of the most creative and best promotions a dealership had ever produced.

For two weeks, Sheehan Buick was transformed into "Camp Sheehan," a make-believe U.S. Army base. The showroom was transformed into an Army garrison, the sales offices were marked as "recruiting" and "discharge" stations, and the telephone operator became the "communications center." The service department was included in the promotion and was appropriately renamed the "motor pool." During the two-week promotion, the entire dealership staff dressed in army fatigue uniforms. The Army was contacted and a local recruiter's office was temporarily moved into the showroom. The Army also cooperated by loaning several military vehicles that were placed on display around the dealership.

Sheehan's replacement during his absence was an absolute stroke of genius. Serving as temporary Commanding Officer of Camp Sheehan was Maurice Gosfield. At that time, Gosfield was better known as the pathetic but good natured Private Dwaine Doberman from the popular television series, *Sgt. Bilko*. In 1959, Gosfield was recognizable to every television viewer in the nation. Sheehan also felt that more could be accomplished with a theme built around the Army character of Doberman than any other media personality.

Newspaper, radio, and television ads announced that Private Doberman was the temporary Commander of Camp Sheehan. He was there to "recruit" all used cars in town with the highest possible trades. Doberman would also be "discharging" all brand new 1959 Buicks. Every sales contract would be personally signed by Private Doberman and anyone wishing to meet the new commander should drop by anytime. For the two-week

promotion, Gosfield was given a new Buick convertible to drive. Keeping with the military theme, the sides of the car were marked with five stars and "Camp Sheehan" flags flew from the front fenders.

Gosfield cooperated by playing his role of Doberman to perfection. He was a warm and pleasing representative in the showroom. Gosfield even did radio and television advertising for the promotion. In addition, he made several personal appearances for publicity.

Despite one week of torrential rains in the area during the promotion, the public turned out to see Private Doberman and buy Buicks. Two hundred cars were sold during Sheehan's successful Doberman promotion. Bringing in a personality as a promotional drawing card was nothing new. But Sheehan's concept to build an entire theme around a personality was an innovation. Newspaper, radio, and television advertising ensured the promotion's success. Sheehan always encouraged inventive promotions, one reason he was the nation's third largest Buick dealer in 1959.

In 1959, Jack Whiteside was the advertising and promotion manager for Polk Chevrolet in Baton Rouge, Louisiana. The dealership was nearing its first year

Annual civic events allow local dealers to display their cars and meet the public. Here, a large tent has been set up for the display of new Buick and Ford models during the 1950 Grape Day celebration in Escondido, California. These gatherings provided an excellent environment to display cars to the community. The people viewing the cars are generally in a festive mood and don't feel the pressure that they might in a dealer's showroom. *Escondido Historical Society*

anniversary and Whiteside wanted to make the event a special occasion. A conversation with a customer was the spark necessary to light off a special first anniversary celebration for Polk Chevrolet. The customer was a square dancing enthusiast and informed Whiteside that several hundred dancers lived in the area and that they maintained a close relationship with other groups in neighboring cities and states. The customer's enthusiasm and numbers of dancers caught hold of Whiteside and he developed a promotional plan for the dealership.

Whiteside's initial idea was for Polk Chevrolet to sponsor a half-hour televised square dance. What Whiteside ended up with was a convention and square dance festival of the South Louisiana Square Dance Council. Instead of 20 or 30 dancers, Whiteside had 200 dancers from Louisiana, Texas, Mississippi, and Alabama. The weekend event turned into a civic event as well, with the mayor proclaiming Saturday as official Square Dance Day in Baton Rouge. A parade was held with Polk furnishing new cars for the officials and flat-bed trucks for the dance groups. A live radio broadcast originated from the floor of the showroom all day Saturday. Whiteside

Most dealers had big events during new car introduction, but a few had colossal celebrations. Jim DiBari, owner of Melrose Motors, spared no expense for the annual event. He not only decorated his dealership's showroom, but also the entire service department. The floors were waxed, banners were hung, and the festivities were kicked off with a marching band. *Charlie DiBari collection*

When the 1956 DeSoto was introduced at Melrose Motors, owner Jim DiBari pulled out all the stops. The new DeSoto sat roped off on a raised carpeted platform in the service department. Eight youngsters in white custom-tailored Melrose Motors coveralls swarmed around, over, and in the car dusting and polishing. The new car introductions at DiBari's Melrose Motors were always big events. *Charlie DiBari collection*

made sure the dealership was the central meeting location for all the dancers. The dancers mingling on the showroom floor in their bright costumes created a carnival atmosphere that drew the attention of the local media. Advertising copy proclaimed that "Polk Chevrolet provided wholesome amusement for friends and customers and they were making it possible for everyone to buy a new Chevrolet at a modest down payment and reasonable monthly payments."

Whiteside felt the promotion was a success. The square dancers served as the window dressing to get the message out about Polk's prices and terms. "Many of our competitors offer down payments as low or lower than ours," stated Whiteside. "The buying public becomes inured to low price offerings. By tying our sale in with the sponsorship of the square dance festival celebrating our anniversary, we enhanced its appeal and thus moved 37 units, an accomplishment beyond our expectations."

Today, automobile dealers are still thinking up off-the-wall ways to get attention. Recently, one San Diego, California, dealer concocted a contest that included a local radio station and an amusement park. The grand prize was a new car. All the contestants had to do to win was ride the roller coaster—over and over and over again. It was a "ride 'till you drop contest" that required the contestants to ride the roller coaster non-stop day and night. During the first few days, most of the contestants washed out, unable to stomach the grueling schedule that allowed them only a short time off the roller coaster each hour. At the rate the contestants were dropping out, everyone was sure the contest would end in a few days. These predictions soon changed to, "would it ever end?" Two of the contestants had iron strong wills and rode for over a week. Their dogged determination made them local celebrities on the evening news. The madness finally ended when the dealer, who had gotten much more publicity from this stunt than expected, gave each of them a car.

Promoting Performance Cars

In the early 1960s the horsepower race had just begun. A few dealers sponsored high-performance cars in an effort to attract customers. At Paul McGlone Chevrolet in Detroit, Michigan, salesman Slim Redford gave parts man Tom Szott and a few of his friends the money for the entry fee at the local drag strip. "All he asked us to do was put his name on the side of the car," recalls Szott. "He'd sponsor half a dozen of us to go to the drags. We'd tape a piece of paper to the side of our cars that said 'Slim Redford Racing Team.' He'd be selling all the hot cars off of what we were doing."

Jim Wangers, an account executive with the advertising agency that did promotional work for Pontiac, had an idea. Wangers went to Bunkie Knudsen, general manager of the Pontiac Division, and explained that a series of traveling high-performance workshops at Pontiac dealerships would boost sales. Knudsen's sales manager at Pontiac didn't think it was a good idea and killed the plan. Knudsen loved high-performance cars and knew

During the week of new car introduction, many dealers would have a special salon showing for local businessmen and regular customers. This exclusive invitation–only event would be held the night before opening the doors to the general public.

Wanger's plan was a good idea, but he didn't want to override his sales manager's decision. So he asked Wangers to find a dealer that might be willing to put on some high-performance seminars. Wangers had a short list of three Detroit-area Pontiac dealers who might be interested in his plan. The first two owners he spoke to were only mildly interested in the idea and wanted to think about it. The third dealership he approached was Ace Wilson's Royal Pontiac. "Wilson wouldn't let me leave—he made the decision on the spot to participate," exclaims Wangers. Wangers wanted more from Royal than just the sponsorship of a race car. He knew that if his plan was to be successful, it would take a full commitment from the sales, parts, and service staffs to sell and service Pontiac's line of high-performance cars and options.

Selling the idea to Royal's sales staff wasn't as easy. Most of the salespeople were content selling Bonnevilles to elderly couples and saw no future in high-performance cars. One salesman, however, saw Wanger's vision. "Dick Jesse learned all he could and every night he had five or six people waiting to talk to him, while the other guys stood around," says Wangers. "Jesse could out-product any customer who came in. That's the kind of guy you want selling this product." Dick Jesse took the time to learn every nuance of what Pontiac was selling, from gear ratios to carburetor linkage. "He had customers saying, 'He knows more about this than I'll ever know.' And, nobody asked questions about price."

The rest of Royal's sales staff grew envious of Jesse's success and soon jumped on the bandwagon, learning as much as they could about Pontiac's high-performance offerings. Ace Wilson loved to see his name in lights and *continued on page 82*

Race cars have always been an attraction at car dealerships. In the center of this Chevrolet showroom is a track-ready '56 Chevy. A race car promotion is extremely effective for the performance enthusiast. It demonstrates to the customer that both the manufacturer and dealer are aware of his interest. *Copyright © 1978-1999 GM Corp. Used with permission of GM Media Archives*

Ace Wilson's Royal Pontiac, in Royal Oak, Michigan, built a reputation at the drag strip for having some of the fastest Pontiacs in the Detroit area. The attention they received at the track brought customers into the dealership to buy a new Pontiac. Royal's sales, parts, and service departments were all geared up for the high-performance customer. *Jim Wangers collection*

Melrose Motors, an Oakland, California, Chrysler Plymouth dealer, gained national recognition with its series of Melrose Missile race cars. Melrose owner Jim DiBari is on the right. In the center is Tommy Grove, the tuner and driver of the Missiles. On the left is Charlie DiBari. He convinced his father that they should sponsor race cars. *Charlie DiBari collection*

Grand Spaulding Dodge in Chicago, Illinois, was built around selling muscle cars. Owner Norm ("Mr. Norm") Kraus grew his successful sales, parts, and service staff from the dealership's knowledgeable and enthusiastic customer base. *Norm Kraus collection*

The affection and fond memories that we have for the car dealers of yesteryear have spawned an interest in dealer collectibles equaled only by those who collect gas station memorabilia. Dealer collectibles are more widely varied than those of the petroleum collectors, running the gamut in size from large to small and in price from expensive to downright cheap. Automobile manufacturers mass-produced much of what is being collected, but many of the specialty items were created and produced by the individual dealers themselves.

One of the easiest dealer collectibles to obtain is a vintage new car sales brochure. Virtually anyone who owns a restored collector car has found an original sales brochure for the model they have. These brochures describe in detail each new model and the options available. Vintage new car brochures are used by restoration enthusiasts to verify available options and original color combinations. Produced by the millions, these brochures are one of the best buys in dealer collectibles.

One of the most sought after and popular dealer collectibles is the promo car. These 1/25 scale models were provided to the dealership by the manufacturer and given to customers or displayed in sales offices. First seen in the 1940s, these cars are extremely popular today. Due to construction of inferior plastics, these early model cars have aged poorly. Because of better materials, dealer promos from the 1950s have survived much better and carry a hefty price tag. In the 1960s, the promo models were becoming much more elaborate, with complete interiors and chassis detail. The high cost of doing business ended almost all of the promo models in the 1970s. Today they are available only in the form of specialty cars, like Corvettes and Vipers.

Dealers have produced a wide array of promotional giveaways. Items range from inexpensive key chains, ice scrapers, and match books to the more expensive engraved cigarette lighters.

Vintage new car brochures are one of the easiest dealer collectibles to find. Each is filled with specifications and images of cars that have become classics. It's interesting to note that it wasn't until the mid 1960s that the manufacturers started to use photographs in their brochures instead of illustrations.

Dealer promo models came in a variety of models and colors. They were supplied to the dealerships by the automobile manufacturers. The rising cost of doing business in the mid 1970s ended production on all but a few of the models.

Paper collectors relish finding stationary from a long-defunct dealership. These items are rare finds, because most stationery gets thrown away when the doors are closed.

Some of the most difficult collectibles to locate are awards given to the salespeople for outstanding sales performance, including tie bars, cuff links, pen and pencil sets, and award plaques. Unique men's jewelry was often given to salesmen to promote a new model being released that year. Banners and oversize posters that decorated the showroom walls and windows announcing the new car theme are also prized dealer collectibles. Because each dealer received only one or two of these items, many have not survived. Each year, at new car introductions, each individual dealer created an entirely new set of collectibles. A few items were provided by the factory to promote a theme for the new models, but most of the others were created uniquely by each dealer: paper cups, napkins, place mats, rain hats, window scrapers, and the ever-popular wooden yardstick.

Many owners of restored cars add a piece of dealer memorabilia to their car when they display it at a car show. It adds to the nostalgia evoked by the vehicle and will always bring a comment from observers. New car brochures are among the most popular, especially if the car featured in the brochure is identical to that of the owner. A license plate frame from a well-established dealer is another nice touch for a classic car. A Royal Pontiac, Yenko Chevrolet, or Mr. Norm's Grand Spaulding Dodge license plate frame adds a finishing touch to a GTO, 396SS, or a Dodge Super Bee. And, it's always cool to have your car keys on a vintage dealer key chain.

The biggest and most expensive dealer collectibles are the large lighted signs from the dealership's exterior. These artfully crafted and often neon-lit signs were landmarks in a small town. Because of their physical size and cost, most of these signs are displayed in auto museums or in the large homes of well-to-do collectors with the space to display them and the funds to acquire them.

Future dealer collectibles are as near as the closest showroom. Any limited production specialty car's brochure (Corvette, Viper, or Prowler) will always be in demand. License plate frames from a dealership that specializes in high-performance cars or is owned by a race car driver will always have a certain cachet about them. So hit your local auto mall and start your collection today.

Grand Spaulding Dodge was the home of Mr. Norm's Sport Club, a fraternity of Grand Spaulding customers. Club members were given discounts on cars and parts. Regular gatherings were held in the service department where 300 to 400 people would attend. Entertaining at this event were the Buckinghams, a popular 1960s-era singing group. *Norm Kraus collection*

Mr. Norm's Sport Club newsletter regularly featured photos of car owners and their cars. Here, one of the members stops by the dealership following a successful run at the drag strip. *Norm Kraus collection*

continued from page 76

it was prominently displayed on his successful race cars. "The thrill of seeing a race car only lasted about 10 minutes," says Wangers. The person with the desire to buy a muscle car needed more than someone to write the order and accept the deposit. They were looking for a salesman who knew the product, a service department that was competent to not only repair the cars, but also increase performance. And finally, a new car buyer needed a parts department that knew which high-performance parts were available and could consult with the customer on his specific application. "The dealers who were spending big money on race cars never had the staff to back up what they were doing with the average customer." Total commitment was needed from everyone in order to make a high-performance dealership successful. Within a short time, Royal Pontiac went from selling sedans to librarians to selling GTOs to young bucks who wanted to cruise Woodward Avenue.

Out on the West Coast, cars sponsored by Melrose Motors had been dominating the drag strips in the Super Stock and Factory Experimental ranks. Melrose Motors didn't turn their operation into a speed shop like Royal Pontiac, but they did install a 500-horsepower dynamometer. Their driver and tuner, Tommy Grove, did some work on a few of the local cars, in addition to

Catchy signs and slogans have always been part of the car-buying landscape. Drawing attention to the dealership through clever advertising and something as simple as a colorful sign in the window is a big part of the equation.

Melrose's own race cars. "We just dominated the local scene for selling high-performance cars," says Charlie DiBari. "Young people would just drag their folks along. There weren't insurance problems in those days, it was just a question of buying a car."

In 1968, half of Melrose's business was in Plymouth's hot Road Runner. DiBari became aware that Chrysler would paint production cars any color shown in the fleet color catalog, if a minimum of five cars were ordered. "We ordered five Omaha Orange and five School Bus Yellow Road Runners," says DiBari. "These things came in and they immediately sold. It got to be that any kid who bought a Road Runner had to buy it from Melrose." Chrysler took notice of the success Melrose Motors was having with their specially colored Road Runners and in 1969, Plymouth started offering a full palate of bright colors in addition to the standard hues.

In Chicago, Norm Kraus and his brother Lenny found that selling high-performance cars off their used

car lot made them a lot of money. In 1962 they were approached by a representative of Chrysler about a Dodge franchise. Upon seeing the new line of cars with the Dodge's new Ram Charger engine, Kraus was convinced. He was going to pattern his new car dealership, Grand-Spaulding Dodge, after his successful used car trade by specializing in high-performance cars. "The first 50 cars we ordered were Ram Chargers," says Kraus. "We ordered a couple of regular cars too, you know, station wagons and four doors."

Not long after the dealership opened, Kraus was approached by a service department customer. "Norm, give me a set of plugs and a set of seat belts and I'll put your name on my car—I'm running at the drag strip." Even though Kraus had a high-performance Dodge dealership, he wasn't into the drag racing scene that was blossoming across the nation. "I told my service guys to give him what he wanted. That was on Saturday. On Sunday we started getting calls. 'Your car won! Do you have any of those in stock?' By Monday we delivered five additional cars."

Kraus decided immediately that his dealership would be totally committed to high-performance in all phases of the operation. "Everyone would be involved," says Kraus. "We had to put people in key positions who knew the high-performance market. That's when we used our customer base. We took a look at the people who bought these cars and hired a few of them. We placed the right ones in key positions; most were under 22 years of age." Kraus found it easier to teach these new young employees the business side of the car trade, instead of retraining the regular staff on high-performance. "We taught them how to sell cars and they caught on quickly. They were our eyes and ears to the world. They had the pulse of the street."

Kraus also created Mr. Norm's Sport Club. "Our biggest promotion was the Mr. Norm Sport Club. When you bought a high-performance car from us, you became a member of the Mr. Norm Sport Club." Members were given a card, decals, a six-month subscription to *Drag News*, a free power tune with the purchase of a car, and a 15 percent discount on all parts purchased. In addition, all members received a free monthly bulletin written by one of the customers. Contests were run for club members to bring in new customers. The winner would typically get $100 or a television for bringing in the most customers in a three-month period.

Kraus realized that the entire pricing structure had to change for the club members. If one member found out that another member had paid less for the same car, all hell would have broken loose. "All the customers got to know each other when they came out to see us race, or at the dealership when we had a social night for the Sport Club members," says Kraus. "They would all be mingling together. It would have been *disastrous* if one person got his car for less than another. We'd have had a line of guys beefin'. So we locked in $200 above invoice on all new high-performance cars and we never had a problem."

The social nights at the dealership were big events for Kraus. Hot dogs and sodas were free and a local band would be brought in for entertainment. "We sold cars to the 1960s singing group, The Buckinghams," says Kraus. "We told them we would cut a deal with them when they wanted some stuff done on their cars, if they made a record for us in exchange." The record they made was used in radio advertisements for Grand-Spaulding Dodge. "The Buckinghams played at one of our club parties. It plugged up the whole neighborhood with 300-400 customers—free hot dogs, Cokes, and dancing till midnight."

Royal Pontiac also sponsored high-performance open houses, featuring plenty of food, tune-up clinics, and racing movies. Royal's race cars were on display along with a large exhibit of high-performance Pontiac components available from the parts department. In the 1960s, young men couldn't get enough of high-performance cars.

These dealerships benefited from their high-profile race cars and the solid reputation they built with the people who bought cars from them. Because of the way the customers were treated, they often referred relatives who were looking for a more mainstream car to these dealers. "I can remember kids coming in with their parents and they'd take them over to see the new GTO," says Wangers. "They would end up buying a station wagon or four door, but often with a larger engine or dual exhaust." Kraus also knew a larger market existed out there. "Each high-performance customer had parents and probably a brother or sister who needed a car," says Kraus. "They also had friends and co-workers who needed a car. That's what we wanted—the whole market. Our niche was to get started in high-performance, then we increased volume, and then diversified."

When high insurance costs, emission controls, and the first gas shortage killed the muscle car market in the early 1970s, both dealers survived. Kraus quickly switched to van conversions and Royal retained their standard customer base. The race car and high-performance promotion has benefited any dealer who put his name on the side of a race car. Those who profited most were the dealers who were committed to all areas of the business.

Self-promotion is what being a car dealer is all about. Every Chevy or Ford dealer sells exactly the same Chevy or Ford that every other dealer sells. To get the buyer's attention, it may be a race car with the dealer's name painted on the side, a marching band, a television personality on site, or oscillating searchlights in the night sky. The dealer promotion puts the sizzle in the steak and helps to define a dealer's personality.

Every car salesman's dream is to have a crowd of people like this waiting for the doors to open at new car introduction. The expansion of the import market in the 1970s all but eliminated the large annual new car introductions. The imports were not introduced in the fall of the year as American cars had been for years. To compete, the domestic automakers followed suit, announcing cars as they were ready for the market. *Copyright © 1978-1999 GM Corp. Used with permission of GM Media Archives*

CHAPTER 4

SELLING CARS
SALESMEN AND THE ART OF THE DEAL

Between 1900 and 1920, selling cars was relatively easy. The demand was higher than the supply. And for the 25 years following World War II, it was again a seller's market. The job of a new car salesman was a highly coveted profession. The cars of that era were all distinctively styled and everyone wanted one. As the market grew more competitive, the role of the car salesman took on more importance. Even a former U.S. president contemplated selling cars at one point in his life. In a 1916 letter, Harry Truman informs Bess Wallace, his future wife, that he is pessimistic about the future of a mining venture in which he was involved. To make money in the meantime, he briefly mentions becoming an automobile dealer and asks her not to lose faith in him.

The job of an automobile salesman is to meet and talk convincingly to prospects. Poise and maturity are the qualities needed, along with being a fluent speaker. Salesmen must be able to explain and demonstrate the mechanical features of each automobile in the inventory, which requires the study of product information bulletins to learn the details of the product. The salesman must be able to determine other people's interests, as well as appreciate and talk about those interests. A car salesman must be a good listener and genuinely interested in people. The job of car sales requires excellent organization and follow-up with prospects and customer needs, as well as long hours of hard work. The reward for those long hours is the satisfaction of fulfilling someone's automotive dream and earning a lot of money.

Over the years many surveys have been conducted on the types of people who are the most trusted and what types of professions receive the most respect. Unfortunately, car salesmen have consistently done poorly in both areas, ranking below defense attorneys. But not all car salesmen are showroom sharks. An overwhelming majority are honest, hard-working people who love cars and selling. Like any good salesman, they know that by treating people with respect, they will get additional business. As one dealership owner said, "Business is never bad when the salesmen are good."

As automobile sales increased in the 1950s, so did the need for qualified salesmen. Many manufacturers sent out books and pamphlets to help dealers determine the best-qualified people for the job. Packard Motor Car Company suggested in their book, *Planned Sales Manpower*, to consider appliance salesmen, because they work in a sales environment similar to the automobile dealership. Packard also suggested that door-to-door "brush and cleaner" salesmen would be good car salesmen, because they were accustomed to "going out after business."

At any dealership, the salesman is the point man for the organization. No matter how well the manufacturer builds a car or how elaborate the dealership is, it's down to the one-on-one selling technique for representing that product and the company to the customer. Nothing happens until someone sells something.

Salesmen must build trust in the customer. If a customer has the slightest inkling that the salesman is going to take advantage of them, they will not do business with them and will go to another dealership. The salesmen must be congenial, look customers in the eye, and answer all the customer's questions authoritatively and truthfully. The salesman must be perceived as a good friend or neighbor. To help foster the image of a solid trustworthy family man, one salesman always had photos of his family in the office. It's hard not to trust someone whose kids play little league baseball.

Until recently, selling cars has always been a male-dominated profession. Like other professions that were once held exclusively by men, women have been accepted into these new roles and have improved the character of the profession. The same is true of car sales.

Competitors will have a difficult time luring customers away if a dealership has the right type of people working for them. The salesperson is the point of sale representative for the multi-million dollar automobile manufacturing company that provides cars to the dealership. That dealership employs many people in several ancillary functions that all depend on cars being sold. The salesperson must be aggressive and must be able to convince prospects of all the claims the manufacturer has made for the car it is selling.

The gentleman on the left is Norm Kraus, who in 1968, was the owner of Grand Spaulding Dodge. Kraus, like many dealership owners, found that contests were excellent motivators for the sales staff. In addition, he added "spiffs" (cash incentives) to almost everything the dealership sold. *Norm Kraus collection*

Working the Floor

The schedule for a car sales associate is grueling. A 40-hour work week is unheard of in the world of car sales. Veteran car salesman Nick Koroly says: "The average auto salesman works 50 hours a week, and it's not unusual to put in 75 hours. Nobody works 40 hours, because you have no control over when your customers are going to be here." The sales staff at a dealership is split into two teams, A and B. One week, the A team will work the early shift between 8 A.M. and 2 P.M.; and the B team will start their shift at 2 P.M. and work until closing. During that particular week, the A team will work one day "bell-to-bell," 8 A.M. until closing, and the B team will have the day off. The bell-to-bell day is usually a Tuesday, Wednesday, or Thursday. The B team will cover both days of the weekend. The following week the B team will work the early shift and the A team the late shift. Some dealers alternate A and B team schedules every other day. Most salespeople do not like this schedule, because they

Having an adequate supply of cars to show a customer is something every salesman needs. A big selection of beautiful new cars in an elegant showroom enhances the customer's buying mood. This tony Auburn showroom in Chicago is filled with the latest 1932 models. *Auburn Cord Duesenberg Museum*

A good salesman must know the product he is selling. Every year, changes are made to the cars. The salesman must be able to identify and discuss the benefits of each new feature with the customer. Here, the salesman on the right is pointing out the highlights of this 1938 Ford coupe. *From the collections of Henry Ford Museum & Greenfield Village and Ford Motor Company*

feel that a customer who makes an initial visit to the dealership in the morning is likely to return during that time period. A car salesperson will always accommodate the customer and come in early or stay late to make the sale.

A sales staff will handle customers who walk in the door looking for a car in one of two ways: the "up" system and the "open floor" system. With the "up" system, all salespeople place their names on a rotation list. When a customer walks in the door, whoever is next in rotation is "up" and will greet that customer. It's an efficient and professional way of dealing with new car customers. The "open floor" system is where whoever gets to the cus-

tomer first claims the customer. It has also been called the "open season" system, because of the rush of humanity that the customer faces upon approaching the dealership!

The ideal customer is the person who walks into the dealership, knows exactly what car he or she wants, doesn't have a trade-in, doesn't haggle on price, and pays cash. This type of customer is one-in-a-thousand. Most customers need some kind of assistance in determining the car best suited to their needs and pocketbook. Every car salesperson has developed biases (most unjustified) toward certain types of customers. One of the types they dislike is what they call a "pipe smoker." A pipe smoker is best typified by

the college mathematics professor who will nit pick and agonize over every decimal point on every line of the sales contract. Asians are also seen as being "too analytical" when making a deal for a car. More than once these biases have come back to bite the salesperson.

"Believe it or not, there are some people who drive up to a dealership and most salesmen won't go out and wait on them," says former car salesman Joe Veraldi. "Right away they prejudge people." Veraldi had an experience that forever dispelled the fallacy of prejudging. He was working at a Southern California Chevrolet dealership when a middle-aged woman pulled up in a beat-up car. It was a dealership with an "open floor" system and all the other salesmen scattered. "There wasn't much going on that day and I'd heard all the other salesmen's lies 10 times, so I decided to go out and wait on her. I walked up as she was ratcheting out of her car with a cig-

arette dangling from her lower lip. She looked as rough as the car she drove in—kind of a biker type." Veraldi extended his hand, introduced himself, welcomed her to the dealership, and asked what type of car she was interested in. In a gravelly voice she announced, "I want to buy a Camaro." A couple of the other salesmen giggled while Veraldi showed the lady around the lot. She found a Camaro she liked and Veraldi got the keys for a test drive. The policy was that the salesman drove the car off the lot and took it to a halfway point. Here, the customer took the wheel for the trip back to the dealership. "When we were switching places she says, 'Just to let you know that I'm not wasting your time and I'm really serious, I won the lottery the other day and I want to buy a new Camaro.' I'm thinking to myself, oh yeah, lottery, right," says Veraldi. Then she opened her purse, removed an envelope, and showed him a photocopy of an instant

This incredible, eye-catching showroom display touts the carefree, adventurous virtues of the 1940 Ford DeLuxe station wagon. It may appear odd today that a dealer would go to this extreme to promote a station wagon. But in 1940, this model was Ford's most expensive offering, and dealers gave it special treatment. How far we have come; this hunting scene featuring wildlife and weapons would not be politically correct in today's culture.

A beautiful showroom full of shiny cars won't guarantee sales. Each dealership must hire ambitious salespeople and compensate them well. In addition, the dealership must actively advertise in the local media to bring in potential customers. *Detroit Public Library, The National Automotive History Collection*

winner ticket for $100,000—and a check for $80,000. "I couldn't wait to get back to the dealership!"

Back at the dealership he sat her down in his office and got her a cup of coffee to go with her cigarette. Veraldi took the check and went to see his boss. "Hey boss," said Veraldi with a smile, "I'm going to sell this lady a Camaro right now." His boss asked why he was so sure. "She just won the lottery!" Veraldi's boss, in a sarcastic tone, replied, "Oh yeah, what, fifty bucks?" When Veraldi showed him the check, his hands were shaking. A half-hour later that lady drove out in her brand new Camaro. "Everybody prejudged her," says Veraldi. "She didn't look as though she had 80 cents to her name much less 80 thousand. I'll never forget seeing that check—it was one of the best sales I ever had."

Compensation

Almost all car sales employees are paid a commission on each car they sell. In 1963 one Chevrolet official said, "We have less than 7,000 dealers and nearly 10,000 compensation plans." The compensation (com-

These Packard dealership owners have just finished dinner and are about to light up a cigar. The event is the regional dealer introduction of the new 1952 Packards. At these meetings, the owners got to see the new cars prior to introduction. They also met their fellow dealers to swap lies and war stories.
Ken Stevens collection

these two prices. That amount ranges between 20 and 30 percent. As an example, a well-optioned car in the late 1950s may have had a manufacturer's suggested retail price of $3,000. The dealer invoice for that car might have been in the area of $2,625. The difference of $375 is what the dealership has to work with and on which commission is based. If a salesperson gave the customer $100 off of the window sticker and sold a $3,000 car for $2,900, the amount of profit for the dealer would be $275. If this particular dealer pays its sales staff 25 percent, commission would be $68.75 (25 percent of $275). By reducing the price of the car by $100, the salesperson effectively lost $25 in commission. If this particular salesman sold 12 cars a month (the industry average), he would have made $825, which was an excellent wage for the late 1950s.

Dealers will often have a sliding scale for the commission percentage. The first two cars sold in a month may be at 20 percent. The next four may be at 25 percent and the remaining cars sold that month will be at 30 percent. This commission plan encourages the sales staff to hustle more cars out the door. The more you sell, the more you can make.

Spiffs

"Spiffs" are also available for the sales staff. A spiff is a cash bonus given directly to a sales employee. The spiff may be for selling certain accessories or services with the sale of a new car. It might even be for selling a specific car on the lot, such as a uniquely optioned car or one that has been in the inventory for a long time. Spiffs are paid directly in cash as soon as the deal is closed. To motivate sales staff to absorb as much product knowledge as possible, one Ford dealership sales manager would regularly walk up to members of the sales staff and ask a technical question about any of the new cars they sold, such as, "How many optional transmissions are available on the new Mustang?" The answer was easy if the salesman had read the product sheets distributed by Ford Motor Company. A correct answer was rewarded on the spot with a crisp 5 or 10 dollar bill. The salesman who couldn't answer the question correctly received a withering look that sent him running to the product sheets. Salesmen love to get spiffs. One said, "I made so much money on spiffs that I never had to cash a check to get spending money."

Delivering a new car is a happy event for both the salesman and the customer. Here, the keys to a new Packard are being given to the Padre on the right.
Ken Stevens collection

mission) of a salesperson is determined by the going rate of the competition. Commission rates for car salesmen vary between 20 and 30 percent. One dealer in an area won't want to pay its people any more or less than any other local dealer. One exception is where the employee's income is strictly salary at dealerships that operate a one-price, "no-haggle" car dealership.

Each car that comes into a dealership has two invoices. The window sticker, which is the manufacturer's suggested retail price, and the dealer invoice, which is the price the dealer paid for the car. When a car is sold, the sales employee gets a percentage of the difference between

Contests

The salesmen at Norm Kraus's Grand Spaulding Dodge always wanted cash. "Whenever we had a contest," says Kraus, "they responded and sales went up 30 or 40 percent. In the 1960s, a good car salesman could make $250 to $300 a week. With spiffs and bonuses, that figure could be doubled." Everybody at Grand Spaulding Dodge was on commission. If the salesman missed adding something like undercoating to a new car, the finance manager could sell the customer the undercoating and get the commission that the salesman would have gotten had he written the undercoating sale. "At the next sales meeting," says Kraus, "that salesman would get hammered, because he missed a potential sale!"

Salespeople also love to win sales contests. To stimulate the sales staff, the owner or dealership sales manager creates a sales contest. The prize might be a color TV, a weekend getaway, a Rolex watch, or cash. The competitive nature of salespeople causes them to spring into action.

One such contest for the sales staff consisted of a dart board with balloons. After selling a certain amount of cars in a month, the sales employee had the opportunity to throw a dart at the board and break a balloon for each additional car sold. Within each balloon were cash prizes ranging from $5 to $100.

One of the most outlandish contests was invented and paid for by Chicago-area Dodge dealer, Norm Kraus. While on a trip to New York in the early 1970s, Kraus went to the diamond district and made arrangements to purchase 20 identical rings, 10 for sure, with a possibility of 10 more later. Back at the dealership, he had a brochure printed for the wives and girlfriends of the salesmen. In that brochure was a color photo of the ring and a description of the contest that the dealership was running for the salesmen. Kraus timed the mailing's arrival to coincide with the sales meeting where he would announce the contest. "At 9 A.M. I presented the contest to the salesmen during a staff meeting," recalls Kraus. "They each had to sell 30 cars, retail, within a month. If they sold that amount, their wife or girlfriend would get the diamond ring." Following the meeting, the phone lines were jammed with calls from the wives and girl-

friends, all announcing, "You'd better win that ring for me!" On the final day of the contest, all but one of the salesmen had sold his quota of 30 cars to qualify for the ring. "On the final day I was going home at 9 P.M.," says Kraus. "This one young fella, Al Poncher, was still there. He refused to leave because he had sold only 29 cars and said to me, 'This place is stayin' open! There's no way I can go home unless it's with a ring.' At 11:30 that night he sold his 30th car."

Kraus even made a big production of presenting the rings. He reserved a room at one of Chicago's finer steak houses. He had all the rings sized for each woman and each was beautifully gift-wrapped. The women had been sent a formal invitation to the dinner, with the option of bringing their husband or boyfriend along. "The entire

This well-dressed group of men has gathered at a Detroit-area Packard dealership for a sales meeting. In the 1950s, selling cars was a male-dominated profession. If this photo were taken today, it would look much different. *Ken Stevens collection*

night we completely ignored the salesmen and made a big deal over the contribution the women made to the business," laughs Kraus. At the next sales meeting Kraus pointed out to the staff that selling 30 cars in a month was a realistic target and that it could be accomplished, even without the pressure from home to win a contest.

Sales Tools

To sell cars, a salesman must have a full compliment of tools and an excellent facility in which to work. An attractively designed dealership encourages people to stop and shop. The first impression made by the showroom will also convince a potential customer to stay and look for a car, because they feel comfortable; or leave, if the showroom is uninviting. The showroom must be clean, uncluttered, and filled with attractive shiny cars. Something the sales staff must receive is proper training on the cars being offered. They must have information available on the models, options, and availability of every car the dealership sells. That information has always been distributed by the manufacturer in printed matter and more recently on video tape.

A full rack of product brochures must be readily available for the customer who wants one. A product brochure filled with colorful images allows the customer to dream about the new car and read about options. Attached to that brochure is the salesperson's business card with the dealer's phone number. One thing every salesperson needs is a lot full of cars. As one salesman said, "You can't sell off an empty shelf." Keeping a large inventory of cars is an expensive proposition for any dealer. But having a customer walk out, because the car they wanted to buy wasn't on the lot available for immediate delivery, is an even bigger loss. That customer will drive to the next dealer, looking for the car they had in mind.

The Demo Car

In the past, one of the big perks given to car sales employees was the use of a demonstrator. The first day on the job, the new salesman got to select a new car, from stock, that would be his personal transportation car. "That was your car!" says veteran car salesman, Nick Koroly, who received his first demonstrator in 1954. "If you were qualified to get hired—you got a demonstrator." What a way to start a new job—a free car. Demonstrators selected by a new salesmen were not stripped-down, family sedans, but well-optioned models. Not everyone got a top-of-the-line model. The newer salesmen often were allowed to select a mid-sized sedan. The convertibles and sport coupes were reserved for the dealership's best salesmen who were consistently tops in sales.

Having a demonstrator allowed the salesman to offer an on-the-spot test drive to anyone he might meet at a local restaurant, golf club, or supermarket. Out of the blue someone may ask, "Say, how do you like your new Super-Sixty Power Sport?" The salesman's response would be, "I love it. Would you like to take it for a spin?" Often, getting someone behind the wheel of a new car was enough to make a sale. Today the demonstration car has all but disappeared. The car business has gotten too competitive and the margins are much slimmer, making the demonstrator a sadly missed perk.

The importance of the test drive was brought to bear in an article written in 1927 by Roy Faulkner for *The Accelerator*, a monthly publication issued by the Auburn Company for its distributors, dealers, and salesmen. Mr. Faulkner pointed out that for several years Auburn's advertising campaign slogan had been, "See the new Auburn—ride in it—drive it, and if the car does not sell itself, you will not be asked to buy." He went on to point out that in a recent investigation of 18 Chicago-area Auburn dealers, not one salesman ever asked the prospect to ride in the car during that visit to the dealership. Mr. Faulkner went on to say, "It is our intention to

Sales Office

inaugurate an intensive advertising campaign built around the idea of getting people to ride in Auburn cars, as there is no doubt about it, the law of averages will enable you to sell a certain percentage of every hundred people that ride in and drive Auburn cars, and therefore the more people you get to ride in and drive Auburn cars, the more sales you will make."

The following year, the Auburn Automobile Company came up with several contests that encouraged potential customers to drive a new Auburn. One of these

This drawing from the 1948 General Motors book, *Planning Automobile Dealer Properties*, suggests that the role of the female was to read a magazine while her husband purchased a car. Within a few years, dealers would realize that women were purchasing cars on their own. Many dealerships had special Ladies Nights to tap into this growing market.

The delivery of the first truckload of new models was an exciting event in 1955. These salesmen knew that in a few days their dealership would be hosting a new car introduction. New car introduction was an exciting time for the entire dealership, because many cars were sold the first week. *Robert Palmer collection*

contests pitted dealers in New York, Albany, Hartford, Buffalo, Cleveland, Pittsburgh, Philadelphia, Indianapolis, Milwaukee, St. Louis, Cincinnati, and Fort Wayne against one another in a sales contest. Banners outside these dealerships touted Auburn's "Show Me" Week. The signs also proclaimed "The car itself is the answer," and "Drive the new Auburn and make the car show you." The Buffalo dealership won the contest and the President's Cup by exceeding its weekly sales quota by 300 percent. Not missing a trick, the Buffalo Auburn dealership had a sleek Auburn Speedster roadster drive around the city with a banner that read, "Official Show Me Car." Auburn owners were asked to participate by placing a "Show Me" sticker in the windshield of their car. An ad was placed in the local paper encouraging prospects to flag down any car with a sticker and ask for a demonstration ride. Car owners gave their "passengers" cards that outlined the advantages of the Auburn.

Prizes were also given to individual salesmen for outstanding sales. Ted Marquard of the Cleveland Auburn dealership was the top salesman with 33 cars sold in one week. In second place was Herbert Groff of

The salesman on the left is no doubt describing the features of the new 1955 Ford. If the salesman feels the customer is a good prospect, he may take him out for a drive in a demonstrator. *From the collections of Henry Ford Museum & Greenfield Village and Ford Motor Company*

While men have traditionally done most of the shopping for a car, women make the final decision. As the salesman looks on, the couple in the foreground is discussing the purchase of a used car. She's convinced the '58 Impala would be perfect, while he has his eye on the Corvette.

Indianapolis who sold 22 cars. Auburn's sales philosophy of getting the potential customer behind the wheel of the car was a success.

The Close

Closing the deal—getting the customer's signature on the bottom line of a sales contract—is not always easy. Often a salesman will turn the prospect over to another senior member of the sales staff to help close the deal. When a salesman uses this "turn over close," he shares the commission with the person who helped. At some dealerships, turning over the customer is a business philosophy.

The potential customer may have three or four salespeople giving them the hard sell. These dealers are called "turn over houses," or simply, "T.O." houses.

One of the best ways to close a deal on a new car is by using the "puppy dog" close. "If you've got something you can put 'em in, and they can smell it, taste it, and drive it, chances are they'll buy," says Joe Veraldi. "That's why the puppy dog close always worked." With the puppy dog close, the customer is allowed to take a car off the dealership lot for an extended period of time without a salesperson. The customer can take it home, show it to the spouse or family, and talk about it without the pressure of the sales staff hovering nearby. The "puppy dog"

THE CAR SALESMAN'S LEXICON

BIRD-DOG—A bird-dog is someone not associated with the dealership who hustles business for a car salesman. Bird-dogs refer potential customers to a certain car salesman and upon the sale of a car, receive a referral, or "bird-dog" fee.

BUSHING—A deplorable practice of having a customer pay more for the car than the price that was agreed upon. To confuse, use subterfuge, or claim "computer error" in the computation of figures.

CHOP THE CLOCK—The illegal practice of setting back a car's odometer.

CIRCLE—The wholesale appraised value of a used car. Derived from the practice of circling the figure on the appraisal form.

CLOSING ROOM—A small room or cubicle off of the showroom where a prospect is led to sign a sales contract or look for an avenue of graceful escape.

CURB—When a new car is delivered and driven past the "curb," it's officially sold. It may be phrased as, "I curbed three cars today!"

DAY'S SUPPLY—The relation of inventory to the average amount of cars sold. This figure is important when ordering new cars to keep the lot filled.

HOPE CHEST—A salesman's file that contains a prospect list.

LOW BALL—The unethical practice of quoting a low net price or high trade-in to entice a prospective customer into the dealership.

SPOT DELIVERY—A car that is purchased upon the customer's first visit to the dealership.

SALES STIMULATOR—Fear, pride, or money.

TISSUE—The manufacturer's invoice for a new car.

WAFFLE—A sales tactic used to confuse a potential customer. When this seldom-successful sales method is used, many cars are shown and many prices are quoted in an effort to bewilder and wear down a prospect.

WOOJATAKE—A tentative trade-in offer stated as a come-on figure. Generally not a genuine proposal, but the customer is given the impression that it's a solid offer.

close gets its name from the phenomenon that takes place in a pet shop when one is faced with a basket full of puppies. Once you pick one up, you won't want to let go.

Prospecting

One of the things any good car salesperson must do is prospect for customers. In 1958, Hodges Auto Sales, a Ferndale, Michigan, Dodge dealer, had been working on a plan

that provided a steady stream of customers and kept its sales staff happy. Sales employees tend to move from dealer to dealer, but Hodges' retention rate was extremely high, with two 25-year veterans and four others with more than 20 years of service. Their motto, "See Hodges for Dodges," was taken quite literally in the Detroit area, where they had delivered 59,000 units in the previous 34 years.

Each morning at 8:30 A.M. Hodges' general sales manager held a meeting to review the previous day's

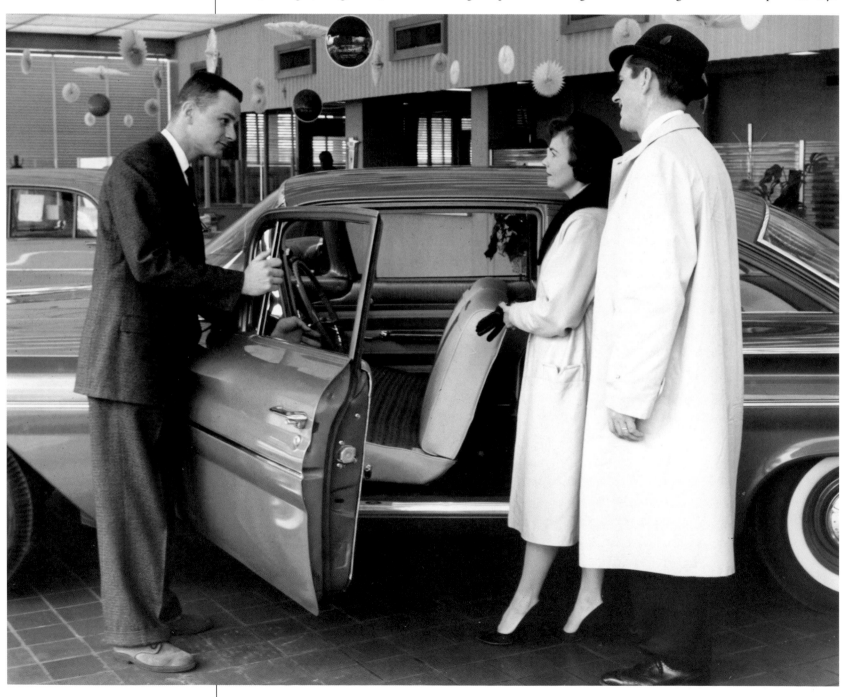

Yes, Mr. Customer, all of your recreational equipment can fit in the back of this new 1961 Olds F-85 station wagon. Salesmen often bring their own sales aids into the showroom to convince customers that the car lives up to its promises. *Copyright © 1978-1999 GM Corp. Used with permission of GM Media Archives*

activities and discuss plans for the day ahead. Hodges had a well-defined prospecting program that contacted 18,200 people each month. Every day, each of Hodges' salespeople were required to mail out a specified number of postcards to potential customers. The postcards did not carry an invitation to visit the showroom, but the prospect was informed that they would be called within three or four days. The purpose of the phone call was to qualify prospects, and they would be asked questions like, "Do you folks want your new car this week or next week?" This rather provocative question, in some instances, revealed the family's intentions. With a positive response, the salesperson had two new objectives. First, to get an appointment and second to discover the wife's favorite color. It was Hodges' belief that the wife was the deciding voice in a majority of car sales. Therefore, an appointment at the potential customer's home was a necessity.

Discovering the wife's favorite color was often a challenge. The salesmen would not ask directly, but they all had their methods of getting this key piece of information. One salesman revealed that if you found out the color of the prospect's living room, it was a good clue in

Car sales employees handle walk-in customers in two ways. In the "up" system, a rotational list of salespeople is made, similar to a baseball team's batting order. Whoever is "up" will approach the next person to walk through the door. With the "open floor" system, the first salesperson to reach the customer works for the sale.
Copyright © 1978-1999 GM Corp. Used with permission of GM Media Archives

Two fully loaded 1964 Chevrolet Impala Super Sport hardtops are in the center of this showroom. These highly optioned models serve as talking points for the sales staff, while discussing a customer's transportation needs. A salesperson with good product knowledge builds confidence in the customer.
Copyright © 1978-1999 GM Corp. Used with permission of GM Media Archives

determining her favorite color. The ingenuity used by the salesmen to determine the elusive shade was often a source of laughs at the next sales meeting.

With a solid prospect qualified and the "right" color determined, the salesman would select a car that most suited what the prospect was looking for and in the color the wife favored. Hodges' salesman preferred an appointment at the prospect's home where the wife could see the car. The deal for the car, however, would never be closed at the customer's house. They would be invited back to the dealership and be introduced to some of Hodges' executives. This "colorful" way of prospecting and selling allowed Hodges Auto Sales to capture 17 percent of the overall Chrysler market in the Detroit area.

Women were not only picking the color of the car in the 1950s, they were also buying new cars. In 1955, 20 million licensed women drivers were on the road. Surveys were showing that in addition to driving, they were also purchasing automotive service and items such as tires and batteries. The traditionally masculine role of car buying was starting to shift. Dealers and the predominately male sales force had to make a few adjustments to appeal to this emerging customer base.

To appeal to female customers, many dealers offered a free copy of Charlotte Montgomery's *Handbook for the Woman Driver*. It covered every phase of car care and use. Some dealers even had special Ladies Nights, serving refreshments and featuring a fashion show in the showroom. Dealers would go as far as tying in sport clothes with convertibles, casual clothes with station wagons, and evening clothes with a sleek hardtop or convertible. Other local merchants would often participate by donating flower arrangements and cosmetic displays. Salesmen were taught to demonstrate to female customers models loaded with comfort and convenience, featuring options such as automatic transmission, power steering, and power brakes. Demonstrations for women were also built around the sale of accessory options, such as a visor vanity mirror and tissue dispensers. Every effort was made to make women feel comfortable in what had traditionally been a male enclave.

Salesmen had to learn that women were smart shoppers and that they couldn't use the same approach that they would with a male customer. Dealers soon came to realize

that women shoppers were looking for courteous salespeople and spotless facilities. The salesmen of the 1950s had to understand that the women looking for a car were not Lucy and Ethel out on a lark. Women represented a segment of the market that would continue to grow.

The people who have been selling cars for a long time love the business. "One of the joys of this business," says Nick Koroly, "is the camaraderie between the people. We have some spare time and you're able to talk and get involved with the other salespeople. You learn a little something from each of your fellow workers."

The job of selling a car has not gotten any easier. Customers are better informed than ever before, and with the proliferation of enthusiast magazines, the Internet, numerous books and price guides, today's car buyer can get the specifications of any new model and even shop for the lowest price without leaving the house. Consumers can now easily determine the difference between the manufacturer's suggested retail and the dealer's actual cost. But it's still up to the salesperson to show the customer where to sign on the dotted line.

Whenever a manufacturer promotes a national retail sale, such as this 1978 Chevrolet Truckload Sale, they turn it into a gigantic event to get the salespeople pumped up. On this day in April 1978, Chevrolet rented the Michigan International Speedway in Brooklyn, Michigan, for the gathering. Here, four members of the sales staff from a Detroit-area Chevy dealer pose in front of a line of trucks ready to deliver cars for the sale. *Ken Stevens collection*

CHAPTER 5

USED CARS

BEST DEAL ON WHEELS

The first documented used car was Henry Ford's Quadracycle. Ford sold his car to Charles Ainsley of Detroit for $200. Later, when Ainsley sold that car to bicycle dealer A. W. Hall, it became the first used car of record. From that day on, the business of selling automobiles in the United States would happen in two phases. New cars, which when out of fashion or in need of mechanical repair, would soon be sold as used cars. A new car was purchased as a replacement for the used one. By the nature of the business, more used cars than new cars have always been available. And as more new cars were released each year, the inventory of used cars continually grew. How these cars are bought, sold, and traded is a story that continues today.

Used cars have typically been genuine bargains, because the biggest enemy of a new car is depreciation. Buying a used car takes advantage of this price drop, and a good used car can be every bit as reliable as a new car for the first few years of its life. Older used cars, while not having the panache of a new car, have proven to be an even bigger bargain, especially those with low mileage. A well-cared-for used car offers real value to the second owner. With used cars, it's definitely function over form, with the buyer getting the most value for the money in a transportation vehicle.

In the U.S. free enterprise system, the independent businessman has always been able figure out how to make an easy buck. It has traditionally taken only a modest amount of money to get into the used car business, nowhere near the required investment to secure a new car franchise.

It was natural that many of the first used car dealers were former horse traders. Because of their familiarity with mechanisms, many bicycle dealers repaired the early cars and also sold them. Blacksmith shops, once the exclusive domain of the horse and carriage, evolved into repair shops and used car lots. Often, early automobile owners were anxious to get rid of a car with mechanical problems for an extremely low price. Savvy mechanics would then buy the car, fix it, and resell it for a profit.

A memorable year in automotive history, 1919, was the first time that used car sales outpaced new car sales. In the mid 1920s, General Motors developed a plan to reduce the amount of used cars by developing a junking fund. Dealers had to pay $5 into the fund for each new car they ordered. This fund allotted up to $50 for each older car taken in on trade that the dealer junked and helped defray the costs involved when a dealer was required to take an older car in on trade for a new car. The idea of reducing the number of used cars would reappear in the near future when the volume of used cars was so high that dealers were handling more used than new cars.

In 1937, the auto industry was still recovering from the depression of the early 1930s when new car sales took a dramatic plunge. Panic set in as the dealers searched for the source of the problem. Their claim was that there were too many used cars in the market and believed that if the older cars were eliminated, more new cars would be sold.

In 1937, of the approximately 25 million passenger cars on the road, more than half were three to six years old, which meant that the remaining 11 million cars were more than six years old. It was the new car dealer's claim that these cars should be eliminated, thereby stimulating new car sales. In the February 1938 issue of the *NADA Bulletin*, Paul Kent, a Mount Morris, Illinois, dealer proposed eliminating used cars. In an article titled "Plan Would JUNK Worn-Out Used Cars Systematically," he wrote: "The cars more than six years old are the real cause of the ills in the automobile business. Since such cars began to outnumber the new cars manufactured, the dealer has held the bag. In the last few years the manufacturer has begun to realize the bad effect on new car sales." Mr. Kent went on to say, "Cars more than six years old should be put out of commission at the rate of the new cars manufactured—3,500,000 each year." It was Mr. Kent's contention that half of each dealer's used car stock should be junked. He also stated that too much money was being tied up by the dealers in reconditioning these older cars, thereby limiting the amount of money available for good used cars or new car stocks.

In the same month that Mr. Kent's article appeared, another article in the *NADA Bulletin* titled "Industry Junking Plan *a Necessity*" fully laid out a

A lot filled with attractive cars is the principal way used car dealers advertise. This Cadillac dealer's used car lot is exclusively Cadillac and they all look beautiful. The second way of advertising is by word of mouth from satisfied customers. *Copyright © 1978-1999 GM Corp. Used with permission of GM Media Archives*

Most small independent used car dealers began like this one—a few used cars in a vacant lot and a couple of incandescent light bulbs strung above. Just like today, the windshield is used for advertising.

permanent used car junking plan. This article stated seven reasons why such a plan should be implemented:

1. To provide a steady replacement market for new automobiles.
2. To enable manufacturers to operate their plants on a profitable basis.
3. To provide regular, steady employment for automobile workers.
4. To establish and stabilize values on used motor vehicles of each previous year model.
5. To promote highway safety by systematically destroying unsafe, obsolete cars and trucks, which owners will use as long as they are available.
6. To provide automobile retailers a means whereby the final trade-on-trade can be destroyed without financial sacrifice to the dealer.
7. To reduce the heavy stocks of service parts now carried by the manufacturers and dealers.

This plan missed reason number eight—big profits for the new car dealers. It was a selfish and short-sighted plan with one major beneficiary, the new car dealer, leaving out the consumer altogether. At this time, the new car market was mostly a replacement market. In the 1930s, the average first car for most families was a used car. To be able to move up to a new car, they needed the trade-in value of their original car. With this plan, the trade-in value of older cars would be reduced to zero, putting a further burden on the new car market. It also overlooked one of the dealers' major profit centers, the parts department. Providing parts and service to used car owners ultimately leads to a new car sale.

Dealer panic over the used car epidemic soon evaporated when new car sales improved in the late 1930s. Unfortunately, many serviceable cars were destroyed during this short period when the dealer's income was threatened. A similar plan to eliminate older cars from the road was again proposed in 1992. This time, the

The banner states that this is "Detroit's Largest & Finest Used Car Market." Most used car dealers never had the money it took to have an indoor facility, especially one that would accept a large inventory of cars, like this one. *Copyright © 1978-1999 GM Corp. Used with permission of GM Media Archives*

The surface of this Oldsmobile used car lot is gravel. Most used car dealers in the 1920s and 1930s could not afford to have their lots paved. This dealer did put a considerable amount of money into the attractive light posts and picket fence surrounding the lot. *Copyright © 1978-1999 GM Corp. Used with permission of GM Media Archives*

focus was on cleaning up the environment by removing older cars with less efficient emission systems.

At the start of World War II, all domestic auto production was halted on February 9, 1942. Car rationing began on March 2. The few new cars that were being built (139 in 1943, 610 in 1944, and 700 in 1945) were conscripted into military service. The industry that had been building automobiles at a rate of four million a year reduced production to zero. Servicemen leaving home put their cars up on blocks or loaned them to relatives. With no new cars being built, America turned to used cars. Used cars quickly became a hot property during the war, so much so that Congress placed ceilings on used car prices. Many of the better financed dealerships bought as many cars as they could find, even from competing lots. It was a seller's market. It wasn't unusual for someone who didn't truly need a car or have the gas to drive it to sell it for a large profit. Stories of people being stopped on the street and offered double what they originally paid for their car were not uncommon. Many of the people who were at home working in the defense industry needed a car and were willing to pay a premium for a good used car. Also at this time, many cars were

pulled out of junkyards and brought back to life. The new car dealers who survived did so by focusing on their used car business and by turning up their efforts on parts and service.

In 1945, 48 percent of all cars in use were more than seven years old. Wartime price controls were lifted on November 9, 1946, and the automobile business boomed. Servicemen returning home reconditioned the older cars they had stashed away. They also purchased used cars in high numbers, since new cars were in short supply while manufacturers tooled up to resume new car production. For each new car manufactured, a dozen people were waiting to purchase it, creating an overflow demand for new cars that brought new entrepreneurs into the used car business.

It was during this time that Norm Kraus and his brother Lenny got into the used car business. In the late 1940s, the Kraus brothers worked at their father's Chicago-area gas station, pumping gas, washing cars, and changing oil. "One of our customers sold us a car for $30 and we sold it for $55—that was the beginning," says Kraus. "We figured it was better than making 3 cents on a gallon of gasoline or washing a car for 75

cents." A couple of the station's customers were used car dealers in Chicago. They helped the boys with their fledgling business and sold them inexpensive cars. "We started fixing up 'bagels,' " says Kraus. "A bagel is a car that's not a completely broken-down rat trap. If it runs good, you can patch the seat or repair a dent on the fender." At that time the brothers were paying between $25 and $100 for their cars. They were helping the guys with the bigger used car lots by taking the low-priced cars they didn't want. Their father's gas station bays were now used to do the repair work on these cars.

"We were at the bottom of the barrel," says Kraus. "We kept learning more about the car business and had a good turnover with the bagels. Everybody starts off in the business with inexpensive cars." Because of their gas station repair experience, the Kraus brothers had a good handle on the cost of fixing the cars they acquired, which allowed them to occasionally double their money on a car. "Selling a car and making $30 profit was a lot of money at that time. "Sometimes we would buy a car and only have $100 in it and then sell it for $195." In the early 1950s, it was big money for two men barely out of their teens.

This small Chevrolet used car lot has just enough props to be considered a used car dealer: a sign, a few strings of lights, and a small office. Many new car dealers felt that the used car side of the business was the ugly stepchild they were required to support, and they rarely put any money into the operation. *Copyright © 1978-1999 GM Corp. Used with permission of GM Media Archives*

In the early 1930s, as the economy sagged, the entire car business struggled for sales. Both new and used car dealers had to find new ways of marketing their cars. This Oldsmobile lot features Safety Tested cars. The safety tested theme is repeated in the large arrow-shaped neon sign. *Copyright © 1978-1999 GM Corp. Used with permission of GM Media Archives*

Functionality and price are the leading factors that go into a customer's selection of a used car. In general, used car shoppers are looking for a reliable transportation vehicle. Here, the salesman on the right is pointing out the features on his stock of used coupes, sedans, and roadsters. *Copyright © 1978-1999 GM Corp. Used with permission of GM Media Archives*

These gentlemen are not reconditioning this used car, but decommissioning it. In the mid 1920s and again in 1937, many used cars were destroyed in an effort to boost new car sales. The theory was that if fewer used cars were available to buy, more new cars would be sold. *Copyright © 1978-1999 GM Corp. Used with permission of GM Media Archives*

In 1951, the Kraus brothers bought a lot adjacent to their father's gas station and moved into the used car business full time. "We had to have a license," recalls Kraus, "that cost us $50. You had to show the Secretary of State that you had a lot, a toilet, a set of lights, and a sign. If you didn't have any felonies, you were okay and could get a license." The Kraus brothers were starting to get repeat customers. "The people who were buying low-priced cars from us were coming back looking for a better car. We were always pushed up by our customer base." The Kraus brothers' success was a combination of timing and hard work. When they entered the car business, automobiles, both new and used, were in demand. The highway system was expanding and more and more people were moving to the suburbs. As their lot expanded, so did their need for a place to do their own reconditioning. They used a small building on the lot to do mechanical repair and body work, but they still used the gas station's bays for minor repair. To supplement their stock of cars, they learned about buying cars at auction.

Cars sold at auction were usually in need of some repair. They were often cars that had been repossessed and were being sold by the finance company. Others were used cars taken in on trade by other dealers who wanted to dispose of them quickly. The final group of cars found at auctions are former fleet cars, including former taxis, police cars, municipal pool cars, and often rental cars. Auctions are for dealers only, but a few public auctions are held. Cars sold at these public auctions are usually "bagels." The majority of cars sold at auction range in age from 2 to 10 years. A sharp buyer could get an inexpensive used car, but those not so savvy ended up with useless junk at these no-return, no-guarantee auctions.

Used car dealers have had a reputation over the years as being unscrupulous. In many instances the reputation is deserved. The used car business isn't the type of business that most people get into for the long haul. To get a license isn't a difficult process. Unlike a new car dealership that has many services to sell a customer, the used car dealer has only one product, the used car. No parts to sell, no oil changes, and no accessories meant the dealer had only the car on the lot, and the customer either bought the car or looked elsewhere. The customers coming in were looking for a bargain and were typically wary of the seller.

Unlike a new car dealer who enjoys the support of a major manufacturer, used car dealers cannot depend on anyone else to tout the features of the cars on their lot. Each dealership is responsible for its own marketing and advertising. Most of the used car dealer's small

This large sign for the Mack-Gratiot Company is illuminated at night by the four light fixtures attached to the top. "Used Cars With An OK That Counts" refers to Chevrolet's used car OK checklist. Below the sign are triangular "sale" banners that attract attention because of their movement. *Copyright © 1978-1999 GM Corp. Used with permission of GM Media Archives*

One of the largest and most inexpensive signs for a used car lot is one that can be painted on the wall of an adjacent building. This Chevrolet used car lot went so far as to paint two other walls, giving their signage additional height. Illumination for this dealership comes from floodlights mounted on poles and on the building wall. *Copyright © 1978-1999 GM Corp. Used with permission of GM Media Archives*

advertising budget will be spent on local newspaper ads. An 1/8- or 1/4-page column ad may be purchased in the automotive section of the want ads or individual ads for specific cars might be placed. These ads need to be cleverly written to get the most impact in the fewest amount of words. The idea is to get a prospective customer interested enough to come by the lot. Once there, the salespeople will work their magic.

Tom Geiman, a used car lot owner in Escondido, California, shies away from too much advertising. "We don't spend a lot of money on advertising," says Geiman. "We take that money and put it into the cars. I want to make sure my cars are a notch better than the competition. Most dealers don't go the extra step. Sometimes you end up with a couple hundred more in the car. But, if the car looks nice, you can ask more for it and it will sell quicker."

For many years, used cars were simply parked on a lot with a sign and a string of lights. The lots were not inviting places to do business. Many new car dealers felt their used cars were a secondary product line and never put much money into marketing these cars. The automobile manufacturers, however, were aware of the bigger picture. They realized that their dealer's success was in part tied to used car turnover. They often suggested ways

continued on page 115

Sun Motor Sales used a combination of dazzling signs, sparkling lights, and a good selection of cars to attract the customer's attention. The two large signs are illuminated with neon tubes, and the sign over the brick office contains a clock. Neon is also used to ring two sides of the lot. Above the cars are strings of incandescent light bulbs. Signs with two arrows invite customers to drive into the lot. Now if they could only do something about the ankle-deep snow. *Copyright © 1978-1999 GM Corp. Used with permission of GM Media Archives*

Used car dealers generally do not purchase used cars outright (unless they are a bargain), but they rarely turn down a trade-in. The trade-in allows them to move another car off the lot. If the trade-in is not up to the quality of the dealer's general stock, it will be wholesaled out to another used car dealer. *Copyright © 1978-1999 GM Corp. Used with permission of GM Media Archives*

The used car operation attached to a new car dealership is required to take in trades. Most of the cars traded in are of the same make as the new cars being sold, especially in the days when customers had a great deal of brand loyalty. If not the same make, the cars traded are in the same price class. This Lincoln-Mercury dealer has a good selection of used Lincolns and Mercurys, along with a nice Buick hardtop. *From the collections of Henry Ford Museum & Greenfield Village and Ford Motor Company*

Every vehicle that comes into a used car dealer is appraised for its current market value. The appraiser must know the local market and have a good knowledge of all makes and models of cars. Every used car dealer is in business to turn cars over quickly for a good profit.
Copyright © 1978-1999 GM Corp. Used with permission of GM Media Archives

Once a used car has been taken on trade, it must be reconditioned before being put on the lot. Reconditioning can be as simple as a good washing, or as complex as a complete engine rebuild. Keeping a used car clean, even in the middle of winter, is important, because it's the first impression the customer has of the car and of the dealership.
Copyright © 1978-1999 GM Corp. Used with permission of GM Media Archives

Continued from page 111

to enhance the dealer's used car operation and this included marketing.

One of the best marketing tools a used car dealer has is the lot on which the cars are parked. A well-stocked lot provides a constant advertisement for the used car business, similar to the way an attractive indoor showroom provides a continual sales pitch for new cars. In fact, a well-planned used car lot can increase customer traffic and the turnover of cars. In the 1950s, these "outdoor showrooms" became more inviting places. Many of the former gravel lots were paved. The temporary looking sales shack was replaced with a more steadfast structure. The small string of light bulbs strung around the lot was enhanced by larger, permanent light poles. The placement and the color of the cars was also important. Similar to the way in which department stores decorate their windows to attract customers, the used car dealers must use the placement of

the cars on the lot to merchandise them effectively. Varying light and dark cars throughout the entire lot will catch the customer's eye.

The windshield of one or several cars on the lot is often marked with poster paint denoting a special option that cars may have or a special price. It's virtually impossible to ignore what has been written on a car's windshield. Then the cars' antennas are decorated with flags and colorful banners are strung across the lot. The waving flags and banners are there to animate an otherwise static display. One important rule for any used car lot is to be sure that the cars are clean at all times.

One of the biggest changes to the used car lot panorama was the addition of covered displays. Large carport-like structures were built to cover as many as 20 cars. These structures were built along the street to shelter the best vehicles on the lot. The long front fascia of the roof was used for additional signage. This protected used car display became a "silent salesman," attracting

Independent used car lots deal in all makes, models, and years of cars. Old cars in poor condition are called "bagels." Dealers who handle these cars make necessary repairs to make the cars salable. Because of their low overhead, independent used car dealers usually sell their cars for less than the used car operations at a new car dealer. *Wendell Snowden collection*

The slightest breeze will set this entire used car lot display into motion. Every trick in the book is used to attract the attention of passing motorists. Red, white, and blue streamers flutter in the breeze between the overhead lights. Between each car in the front row are flags. Even the light pole at the entrance is painted like a barber pole in red and white. *From the collections of Ford Motor Company*

This Ford dealer has placed its used car lot on the corner, and directly behind it is the service department and the new car showroom. New car dealerships used their service department staff to recondition used cars, which lowered their cost of reconditioning. *Escondido Historical Society*

customers to stop in and walk around. The covering offered protection from the weather for both cars and customers, giving the cars a cared-for look. On the hottest summer days, the cars would be shaded and the customers would be encouraged to browse longer. A potential customer would be more inclined to test drive a car that had been parked in the shade over one that had been sitting in the sun. Rainy days are typically the slowest for used car customer traffic. The covered display made these formerly slow days more productive. Protecting cars from the elements turned out to be a blessing for the Rambler Auto Clinic in Rapid City, South Dakota, in 1963. One month after installing a covered area for 16 of its used cars, a severe hailstorm hit the area. The covered cars were protected from costly damage.

The construction of these covers was as easy as building a carport—a simple framework of structural steel covered by translucent panels overhead. The translucent panels allowed light to filter through during the day and provided a reflective background for the network of lights installed under the covering for evening illumination. Quite often, because of the well-lit display, nighttime browsers would return as daytime customers.

Dealers soon found that a covered used car area transformed their ordinary lot into an attractive outdoor showroom. When Halladay Motors, an Oldsmobile dealer in Cheyenne, Wyoming, installed a covering over the used car lot in 1964, it improved the image of

Committing capital to used car inventory is a decision any car dealer must make. This investment of capital is more crucial for the small used car dealer than it is for the large new car dealer, who may be able to better weather the slow periods. The small operator must turn cars over quickly to stay in business. A 30-day inventory of cars is optimum. Anything more than that can be fatal and anything less is a bonus. Moving cars quickly is the name of the game. Winning this game depends on how well the dealer executes three objectives: appraisals, reconditioning, and sales.

An appraisal is the process used to determine the trade-in value of a used car. The amount of profit or loss in an automobile sale hinges on the appraisal. One rule of thumb followed by all dealers regarding appraisals is to assign the task of appraisal to someone not connected with a pending sale. Otherwise, the appraisal may come in too high in an effort to clinch the deal on the newer car being purchased.

The appraiser must be able to make a series of decisions and evaluations quickly and accurately. Both the salesperson and customer should not have to wait an extended period of time. Appraising is a tightrope act where a low appraisal may hurt a new car sale and a high appraisal will create a problem for the future sale of the car. Appraisals are done by the dealership's most experienced staff members. These people must be knowledgeable on all makes of cars and know the local market conditions. They must know the models and options so they don't get fooled on a trade-in or inadvertently misrepresent one of their products. The appraiser must be familiar with reconditioning costs and keep in mind that a balanced inventory on the used car lot is important.

Many used car dealerships use an appraisal form with as many as 25 individual items to be surveyed. With this checklist, the appraiser is less likely to overlook any important areas. This form may be broken down into the following categories: body, chassis, engine, and interior. The body is checked for any visual damage or repair work. Overlooking a poorly repaired fender that needs to be redone might kill any potential profit. On smaller independently owned used car lots, the owner will do all the appraising and just run through a mental check list and then go on gut instinct. Independent used

the entire operation. They also noticed an increase in sales when their usual 25-day supply of used cars dropped to 18 days.

Some dealers have gone one step further by having an indoor showroom. Indoor used car showrooms are typically used to display late model upscale used cars. These indoor showrooms offer the customer the maximum in viewing comfort. To promote test drives, the used car showroom must be designed with stalls and aisles arranged to make vehicle circulation appear easy. If not, customers might not ask for a demonstration drive, feeling that such a request might obligate them to buy the car or otherwise inconvenience the dealership.

continued on page 123

For decades the OK used car sign has been a landmark for someone looking for a quality used Chevrolet car or truck. The cars under the OK sign were safety checked, fully reconditioned, and received a warranty. *Copyright © 1978-1999 GM Corp. Used with permission of GM Media Archives*

You've a lot to look for under our sign

More than just an ordinary used car lot.

For one thing, you'll find an extraordinary selection of used Chevies and other makes. From convertibles to pickup trucks. All with plenty of unused miles.

For another, you'll meet an experienced salesman who's also a used car specialist. When you ask questions, he'll give you straight answers—the kind of answers that will help

you make a good choice when you buy.

And, just as if you'd bought a new car, your Chevy dealer's highly trained service staff is there to help you if you ever need it.

So, when you're thinking of buying a good used car or a serviceable truck, remember your Chevrolet dealer's OK sign. It stands for a lot.... Chevrolet Division of General Motors, Detroit, Michigan.

Chevrolet new car sales were so good in the early and mid 1960s that they placed full-page color ads in major magazines for their used cars. Chevrolet cars traditionally held their resale value and moved off the lots quickly.

USED CAR WARRANTIES

In an effort to increase consumer confidence in their used cars and to move them off the lot, dealers for the major auto manufacturers warranted their used cars through their authorized dealers. The Chevrolet plan was called the OK Used Car Warranty, Ford's plan was called the A-1 Used Car Warranty, and Lincoln-Mercury had their Silver Crest and Gold Crest Warranties. Under these arrangements, the dealer selling the car accepted responsibility for up to 50 percent of the cost of parts and labor for any repairs needed during the first 30 days. For the next two years, the dealer picked up 15 percent of the cost of repairs. Under most used car warranties, the repairs had to be made by the issuing dealer's repair facility and at the standard retail price.

Participating dealers pledged that all used cars would be honestly represented, fairly priced, and in good condition. The dealer also gave the buyer a written promise that each

The Chevrolet OK used car logo has become almost as recognizable as the Chevrolet bow tie. Initiated in the 1930s as a quality check program, it eventually grew into a guarantee plan. *Copyright © 1978-1999 GM Corp. Used with permission of GM Media Archives*

car had been inspected, road tested, and that necessary repairs had been made prior to the sale. Excluded from most used car warranties were tires, tubes, glass, radio, air conditioners, and any damage due to an accident or misuse. Some warranties made tires available at a 25 percent discount during the first 30-day period only.

One of the best automotive bargains to be found on a used car lot is a vehicle that is still covered under the

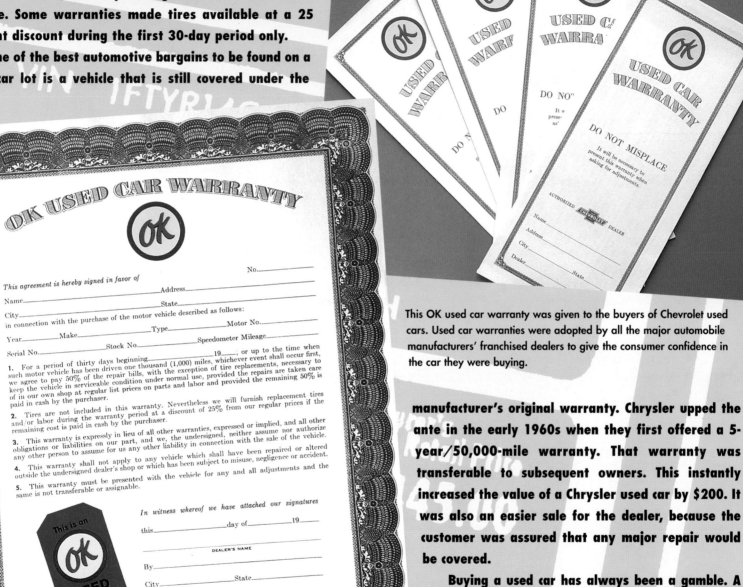

This OK used car warranty was given to the buyers of Chevrolet used cars. Used car warranties were adopted by all the major automobile manufacturers' franchised dealers to give the consumer confidence in the car they were buying.

manufacturer's original warranty. Chrysler upped the ante in the early 1960s when they first offered a 5-year/50,000-mile warranty. That warranty was transferable to subsequent owners. This instantly increased the value of a Chrysler used car by $200. It was also an easier sale for the dealer, because the customer was assured that any major repair would be covered.

Buying a used car has always been a gamble. A lemon could cost the owner a fortune in repairs, turning an inexpensive transportation car into a headache. Used car warranties sponsored by the major automakers helped relieve the buyer's anxiety and made the cars easier to sell.

When a used car dealer takes in a car on trade that may not fit the dealer's profile of cars, they will often trade the car or wholesale it to another used car dealer. To the left of the used car office is a Lincoln Continental Mark II. It's unusual to see a car like this on an Oldsmobile used car lot, because it's a Ford Motor Company product at the high end of the luxury scale. *Copyright © 1978-1999 GM Corp. Used with permission of GM Media Archives*

Used car dealers attract attention by the way they display their cars. The cars in the front row on Charnock Oldsmobile's used car lot are all in shades of red, white, or blue. A front row of cars painted the same color would not catch the eye of someone driving by. *Copyright © 1978-1999 GM Corp. Used with permission of GM Media Archives*

Continued from page 118

car lot owner Tom Geiman quipped, "Sometimes you just don't feel comfortable trading whatever they have, so you pass." Years in the business give these owners a feeling for a car's value and if someone is trying to pull a fast one.

Quite often, people who are basically honest and upstanding citizens will do their utmost to get the best of a used car salesman. Even sweet little old ladies turn into cunning adversaries, because they are sure they are going to be cheated by the fast-talking used car salesman. As the customer approaches the dealership, a mantra of "I'll cheat him before he cheats me" can be heard softly chanted. Almost every used car salesman has a story of a customer who tried to dupe him on a used car trade-in by removing all the serviceable components. The day following an appraisal, the customer would bring the car back with a set of bald tires, a radio that didn't work, and a dead battery—none of which were on the vehicle when appraised the day before. More often than not, the sharp used car buyer will catch the customer's tricks. That customer's chance of getting a good deal or a special price on another car on that lot has now evaporated.

Many used car dealers have taken the rap for what a few unscrupulous ones have done in the past. Many have regrooved tires, used excess body putty to fill in holes and dents, used heavy oil in the transmission or differential, or set back the odometer. One of the most

Ace Auto is a used car dealer that deals exclusively in "bagels"—inexpensive transportation cars. Either of these two beauties could be driven off the lot for $750.

common lines given to used car salesmen is, "I know how you dealers are." Norm Kraus's response to that statement would be, "Do you know *me*? Did I ever sell *you* a car? Then how do you know *how* I am?" Most of the time the customer mentions what happened at another lot or repeats a rumor he heard once about used car salesmen. Because bad news travels faster than good news, used car dealers are reluctant to try these old tricks anymore.

Once a used car is taken in, it must be reconditioned before being put on the lot. The dealer wants this process to happen as quickly and as inexpensively as possible. The sooner the car is on the lot, the sooner it can be sold. And every dollar saved in reconditioning is an additional dollar in the dealer's pocket. As one used car dealer so eloquently stated, "Appearance sells 'em, but mechanical reconditioning keeps 'em sold."

The first step in used car reconditioning is a thorough washing, which includes removal of seats and carpet. The

Independent used car dealers rely more on attractive pricing than do the lots associated with large new car dealerships. Often, several independent used car dealers are located along the same street where they must compete with large bright signs for the attention of customers.

ashtray, glove box, and trunk must be spotless, and the engine compartment gets a complete steam cleaning. Any trailer hitches or unique accessories added by the former owner must be removed. If left in place, this type of non-standard equipment will raise unnecessary questions in a prospective buyer's mind (i.e., Did someone try and tow a boat with this Corvair?).

The final steps in the reconditioning process are body and mechanical repairs. Often a used grille or hood is a sufficient replacement for a used car and will save the dealer money. A reputable used car dealer can't afford to sell a car that is unsafe to drive. All necessary mechanical repairs are made to make sure the new owner will have no problems.

At the time the car is taken in, a decision must be made whether to keep the car, recondition it and place it in the used car inventory, or to wholesale it to another dealer. Wholesaling is done to dispose of a car that is in need of too much work to be reconditioned. Another reason to wholesale a car is to maintain an inventory balance on a lot. A used car lot with three or four similar, two-year-old Ford sedans is out of balance. One or two of these cars will be dealt to another used car dealer,

Many new car dealers started out in the automobile business with small used car lots similar to this one. Even though the lot is gravel and does not have any extra lighting, the Cherry Auto Sales facility is neat and the cars look good. The sign is used to advertise this week's special.

Small independent used car dealers cannot afford the lavish signs that the well-financed new car dealers have for their used car lots. Stoney's well-worn, hand-painted sign is reminiscent of the used car dealer signs of the 1920s and 1930s.

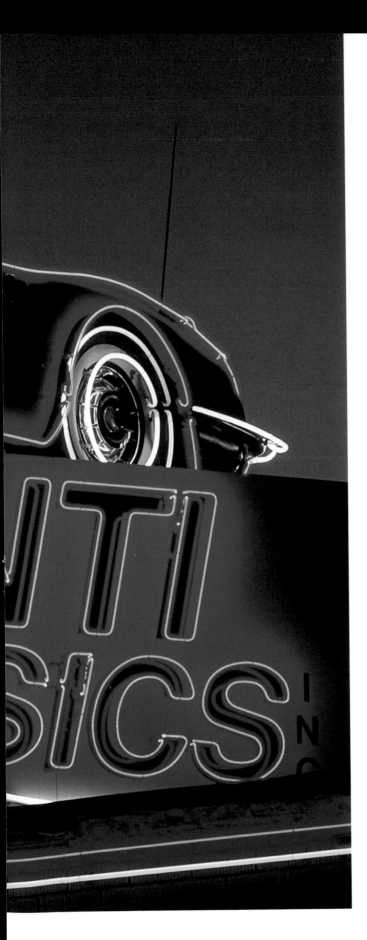

The days of speedometer tampering and vehicle misrepresentation on used car lots is a thing of the past. Today's used car dealers have felt the wave of consumerism that has swept the country and know that they must honestly represent the vehicle being sold. *Howard Ande*

This used car dealer specializes in classic cars. To attract attention, the owners have placed an older Corvette on top of the sign and outlined it with neon lights. *Howard Ande*

Used car dealers have provided Americans with transportation cars for more than a century. Getting into the business is relatively easy. Staying in business requires accurate appraisals, and sales and merchandising skills.

preferably one in another town. Also, each dealer has its own clientele of buyers. A luxury car on the lot of a used car dealer that specializes in transportation vehicles will sit for a long time.

In the early days of used car selling, it wasn't unusual for the dealer to do a little "customizing." Norm Kraus recalls, "We'd buy a clean '53 Chevy two-door 210 sedan," the most inexpensive model Chevy offered in 1953. "Then we'd go to the local Chevy dealer and buy the Bel Air fender script, side moldings, and a set of full wheel covers." They would repaint the sedan in an attractive two-tone paint scheme, add the Bel Air trim and place it on the lot. This type of resourceful used car "merchandising" was one of the inventive ways an independent used car dealer moved inventory. Kraus also remembers a clean, low-mileage four-door they bought. "We had a '54 Pontiac sedan with 18,000 miles on it. The car sat for 30 days and didn't sell. I told my mechanic to pull the speedometer out of the car. I set it to 38,000 and it sold that afternoon. If a customer looks at a car with what appears to be unusually low mileage, they will often think that the speedometer has been turned back and pass on the car."

In used car sales, the condition of the car does the selling. People shopping for a used car usually have a specific budget and a car in mind. A good salesperson can facilitate the deal by pointing out features on a car the customer may have missed, or by offering an attractive alternate car in the same price range. A poor salesperson will surely kill the deal by pressuring the customer.

In the 1950s, Chevrolet cars were proven to be reliable, inexpensive to repair, and attractive. For these reasons, they became the favorite of used car buyers. On the used car lots, the Chevys would always be parked in the front row. Because of the demand, the prices on Chevys were always higher. But, it also cost more to buy the Chevys. The most profitable used cars in the 1950s were Chrysler products. A loaded 1952 Chrysler could be bought for much less than a 1952 Chevy Bel Air. A crafty used car dealer would place a loaded Chrysler next to a Chevy. The customer would be drawn to the Chevy. Once a price was quoted they would be in sticker shock at the price being asked for a transportation car with a stick-six. Sitting near the Chevy would be a Chrysler of the same vintage. The clever salesman would point out that for only $100 more than the Chevy, they could be riding in a luxurious Chrysler. Unbeknownst to the customer, the dealer paid $100 less for the Chrysler than the Chevy. The salesman would get the keys and take the prospective customer for a test drive. The luxury and power of a Chrysler V-8 would win the customer over.

Chevrolet was selling a lot of new cars in the 1960s. As a result, Chevrolet dealers acquired a large number of quality used cars as trade-ins—usually Chevys. Used Chevrolet vehicles held their value better than most of the competition. In 1965, the average used 1962 V-8 Impala sold for $1,625, about 57 percent of the original retail price. By comparison, the average 1962 Ford Galaxie was returning about 51 percent of its original price, a 1962 Dodge only 46 percent. Generally, what's hot in the used car trade today can be traced back two years. Whatever was the hot seller two years ago, will be the hot seller on the used car lots today.

For a century, the buying and selling of used cars has been a part of U.S. landscape. As the new car industry grew, so did the used car market. Small independent used car dealers often started on a shoestring with one or two cars and a dream of being in the car business. Many of these small businesses grew into large new car franchises. Along the way, they provided high-quality inexpensive transportation to the many people who could not afford the American dream of a new car. The used car business will always flourish simply because of the volume of new cars being produced each year.

Used car dealers have realized that the next best thing to an indoor showroom is an outdoor area where the cars are covered, protecting them from the elements. This dealership has also marked the year of manufacture on the windshield of each car.

CHAPTER 6

PARTS AND SERVICE

SERVICE AFTER THE SALE

In the automotive business, the new car and used car sales areas are called the "front end" of the business. The "back end" of the business includes the parts and service areas. It's a well-known adage in the world of car dealers that the front end gets the business, but it's the back end that keeps the business.

Parts and service have always been the backbone of an automobile franchise. When the early automakers struck a deal with a potential franchise holder, one of the first requirements was for the new car dealer to buy an adequate supply of spare parts for the new cars he was about to sell. Because most of the cars the dealer received from the factory needed some assembly, the new dealer quickly became skilled at repair.

Parts Department

When dealership facilities are planned, approximately 10 percent of the total floor space is allocated to the parts department. Parts departments are located near enough to the new car showroom so that the potential new car customer can see that this dealership offers full service. This relative position also allows the parts customer to see the new cars on the showroom floor.

The parts area is typically designed for merchandising appeal, as well as to offer the customer a convenient parts and accessory outlet. When planning a dealership parts department, street and floor traffic must be taken into consideration. The sales displays are most effective if chosen to appeal to the dealership's largest customer base. In the past, automobile dealership parts departments were often visible as part of the store front display or had a parts display window that faced the street.

Two types of buyers frequent a dealer's parts department: retail and wholesale. The retail buyers are those customers who buy parts and accessories to service their own car. Wholesale buyers are independent repair shops and fleet mechanics who buy in quantity.

Retail buyers are drawn to the dealer's parts counter for the genuine factory-manufactured parts and accessories. When they service their car, they want the replacement parts they buy to be of the same quality and fit as the original parts. These retail buyers come into the dealers parts area in person to order and pick up their parts. They generally know what part they need, but will not know the part number. One of the counter employees will look up the part number in one of the massive parts catalogs and either retrieve the part from stock or order it from the warehouse.

Three types of purchases are made by the retail customer at a dealership's parts counter. The "demand sale" is where the customer comes directly to the parts counter looking for a specific part. The "anticipation buy" is made to stock a customer's personal parts bin with oil, fan belts, and gaskets in anticipation of a future repair. Often this type of purchase is made after seeing a display of these items in the parts showroom. The final type of purchase made by the retail customer is an "impulse buy," which can be directly attributed to a display of parts or accessories that attracts the customer's attention.

The parts salesroom display provides the retail buyer with additional parts to satisfy an impulse buy. Items on an attractive open display may be accessories to enhance the appearance of the owner's car. Items like spotlights, fender skirts, fog lights, and mirrors have always been inexpensive and easy to install. Or it may be items such as wax and chrome polish to bring back that new car sparkle. These items are always attractively displayed to catch the customer's eye.

Most dealer parts operations will have two parts counters: one for retail and wholesale customers, and another for the dealership's service department mechanics. At this second counter the mechanics performing warranty work or general repairs can obtain their parts. This counter, which is usually small and often a "Dutch door," is not accessible to the general public and is there only for the convenience of the dealership's in-house mechanics.

The parts department may also have display space in the new car showroom. Here, the accessories that can personalize a customer's new car are put on display. It can be hard for any new car customer to pass up an inexpensive extra from the display. These impulse buys are encouraged by the sales

In the 1960s, dealership parts counters were beginning to look like speed shops. In addition to the standard factory replacement parts, the parts department at Grand Spaulding Dodge sold mag wheels, exhaust headers, and traction bars.
Norm Kraus collection

Keeping an adequate supply of parts on hand was one of the requirements to obtain a franchise to sell Ford cars. Having a tow truck to bring in disabled cars, like this Model T with a crumpled front fender, enhanced the service department's profits. *Detroit Public Library, The National Automotive History Collection*

staff who might point out how convenient a vanity mirror would be for the sun visor. Dealer-added accessories carry high profit margins and the sales staff receive a substantial incentive to sell them.

One of the most unusual accessories ever stocked in an automobile dealership's parts department was charcoal briquettes. In 1924, Ford Motor Company's Iron Mountain facility in Kingsford, Michigan, built the wooden bodies for the company's station wagons. The process of building a wooden auto body produced a tremendous amount of wood chips. Henry Ford hated to see waste of any kind. He knew that money was being swept out the door and something could be made of this byproduct. Some of these chips were carbonized and pressed into charcoal briquettes. Through the 1920s, these briquettes were sold commercially to restaurants, to meat and fish smoking plants, to railroads for the heating of cars, and to homeowners. During the depression when car sales fell, Ford dealers were told to start selling briquettes. Some dealers even carried barbecue grilles.

Service Department

It's the responsibility of the dealership service department to render quality service to car and truck owners at prices that are reasonable to the customer and profitable to the dealer. The automobile dealer service department also provides "internal service" at the lowest possible cost, while keeping quality high.

A well-planned dealership service department will not only assure the maximum use of available space, but will also make a favorable impression on service customers. The service department in any dealership is allotted the most floor space, typically about 73 percent of the total building. The layout of each dealership's service department is designed to function as smoothly as possible. The vehicle service bays (or stalls) are laid out to allow as many bays as possible without impeding normal traffic flow through the service area. Service bays with the easiest access are designated for fast turnover jobs. The noisier and heavier jobs are usually performed in service bays located away from customer traffic.

In 1917, Ford required that its dealers carry a $20,000 parts inventory at all times. This Ford dealer's glass cases are filled with factory-fresh parts. On the top of the shelves in the rear of the department are new tires. Above the archway to the right is a framed portrait of Henry Ford. *From the collections of Henry Ford Museum & Greenfield Village and Ford Motor Company*

Working in the service department of any dealership in the 1920s was hard, dirty work. These Oldsmobile mechanics are doing their best under less than ideal conditions. The only lighting available is from the windows on the left. The two small bare bulbs, scarcely visible in the ceiling, are not turned on. Even if they had been, it would not have provided enough light. *Courtesy Oldsmobile History Center*

Most of the early dealerships were located in buildings that had originally been designed for other uses. The large support pillars in this Oldsmobile dealership service area made movement of the cars difficult. *Courtesy Oldsmobile History Center*

The work assigned in a dealership service area is split into two categories: heavy and light. Heavy work is considered engine removal or replacement, frame repair, suspension repair, or any major repair that would normally take more than one day to accomplish. Heavy repair work is usually tackled by the most experienced and best-trained mechanics. The work typically done in a heavy repair bay is greasy and dirty. Because these heavy repair bays suggest to the customer a lengthy and expensive repair, these bays are placed as far away from the customer waiting areas as possible.

Light repair includes routine tune-ups, oil changes, exterior or interior trim repair, or any work that doesn't require a highly skilled mechanic. By the nature of the work, the light repair bays have the shortest turn-over times and are the easiest to keep clean and orderly with a minimal amount of effort. Many of the specialized electrical diagnostic tools and engine tune-up equipment used in the light repair bays is attractive and impressive. The light repair bays are closest to the service department entry and customer lounge areas.

The service bays are required for all types of work in the dealer's service department. A service bay is a

This photo was taken in 1932 at F. H. Daily Motor Company, a Chevrolet dealer in Oakland, California. In the 1930s, dealership service departments were becoming a more civilized place to work. Large skylights provided plenty of daylight for the mechanics. Individual repair bays were identified with signs, and lines were painted on the floor, giving the area a sense of order. *Copyright © 1978-1999 GM Corp. Used with permission of GM Media Archives*

A body shop was (and still is) an integral part of any automobile dealership. This white-coveralled repairman is using an acetylene torch to weld a rear fender on a 1932 Chevrolet. Behind him is a large cabinet filled with specialized tools for body repair. *Copyright © 1978-1999 GM Corp. Used with permission of GM Media Archives*

well-defined, accessible area large enough to comfortably accommodate one car and the mechanic working on the car and averages 12 feet wide by 24 feet deep. The service lane that gives access to the bays is about 20 feet wide. Usually, the aisles and service bays are marked with painted stripes on the floor. Most service bays are equipped with an exhaust gas control system to allow the car being repaired to be run safely inside the building. These exhaust control systems are built into the shop floor and are connected to the car's exhaust pipe by a flexible, metallic hose that slides into the floor ducts when not in use. Without these systems, the service area would soon fill with smoke and deadly carbon monoxide.

A lubrication bay near a customer reception or lounge area has several important advantages. A well-maintained lubrication bay is an attractive self-merchandiser. The lubrication hoist is an excellent location from which to market extra service work to a prospective customer. The service writer has a captive audience when a customer's car is up on the rack. He can point out the areas on a customer's car that may need some extra service. Nothing sells a front-end alignment better than the customer personally seeing, from under the car, a leaking shock absorber or badly worn tires.

On the left, a customer watches as a technician, seated in his 1932 coupe, adjusts the chassis alignment. Cars of the 1920s and 1930s had primitive chassis and were susceptible to all kinds of shakes and rattles. The dealers had money to buy the most sophisticated equipment available at the time.
Copyright © 1978-1999 GM Corp. Used with permission of GM Media Archives

This Oldsmobile parts department of the early 1930s was probably located within the service department area. Displayed on the ends of the parts bins are commonly used gaskets. On the counter is a display for two "factory approved" heaters. The standard model on the left sold for $11.95 and the deluxe on the right cost $16.75.
Courtesy Oldsmobile History Center

The retail parts department in this Pontiac dealership was designed to let the customer see the components of every system in the car. Around the walls were displays for carburetion, cooling, ignition, transmission, fuel system, brakes, electrical, clutch, and front end. The small displays in the center of the floor carried an array of spot removers, dri-gas, tube repair kits, and polish. *Copyright © 1978-1999 GM Corp. Used with permission of GM Media Archives*

Cars of the 1930s needed more frequent lubrication than cars of today. In addition, many of the lubrication points needed specialized guns (located to the right). On the left, a service writer (in the white shop coat) is trying to sell the customer another service. *Copyright © 1978-1999 GM Corp. Used with permission of GM Media Archives*

This Chevrolet parts department is laid out in "hardware store" fashion, where every part is available to the customer. The vertical rack to the left of the bumpers holds a large selection of running board moldings. Above the bumpers is a display for a grille guard ($6.60 installed) and fog lamps (also $6.60 installed). *Copyright © 1978-1999 GM Corp. Used with permission of GM Media Archives*

The front-end alignment service bay is slightly larger than the regular mechanical bays. It may be built with a shallow pit or a platform. The equipment used to align a car's front end is interesting and imposing to the average customer. For these reasons, the front-end alignment bay is always in an area that has customer access.

The wash rack and new car preparation bays are in an area removed from the service department's regular traffic. The wash bay should be in an area that has a drain and where overspray won't affect work being done on other cars. The new car preparation bay should also be away from customer areas. During preparation, new cars do not look their best and are often handled in a way that may appear rough to the new owner. When the customer first sees his or her new car, it should look impeccable.

The dealer's body and paint shop is usually separate from the service department and, in many cases, is in another remote location. Body work is noisy, annoying, and distracting to other service personnel. The dust and dirt generated by body work can harm other close tolerance repairs in the general service area. Because it's closely related to the body repair shop, the paint shop is usually located within the same building. The unsightly appearance of cars under repair and the hazards of paint and body work make the remote location of these two facilities desirable.

A well-planned customer reception area is an important asset to the service department. The entrance and driveways must be clearly marked. If a customer is favorably impressed upon entering, he or she will be more likely to purchase additional services and carry away a lasting good first impression of the dealership's service area. The service writers who make the initial contact with the customers are also important. They must be congenial and interested in the customer's problems. A surly service writer can turn a customer into a former customer in a matter of minutes. A sharp service writer can spot a potential problem with a customer's car and offer an additional service that might prevent a breakdown on the road. This proactive approach is appreciated by the customer. Service writers must be able to explain to the customer the dealership's service policy, give an estimated cost, and indicate how long it will take to make the requested repairs.

A customer lounge is available for patrons who choose to wait for the service to be completed. This lounge is always located with easy access to the service department, parts department, and new car showroom. The customer lounge is always stocked with an assortment of magazines, a local daily newspaper, and plenty of free coffee. Often dealers will provide other unique distractions to keep the customers busy while waiting. In 1966, a Cadillac dealer in Edina, Minnesota, installed a putting green for customers who were waiting for their cars to be serviced. Today, the dealership customer lounge is nearly always equipped with a television tuned to a cable news network.

In the 1940s, 1950s, and 1960s, some large dealerships maintained the flow of traffic from a control tower. From what looked like a small airport control tower elevated 30 feet over the shop floor, a dispatcher would direct the department's flow of work. The control tower was more prevalent in larger dealerships with multiple service bays and a high volume of activity. In front of the dispatcher were the service orders for every vehicle in the shop. He

This Little Rock, Arkansas, Chevrolet dealer's service area provided a clean well-organized atmosphere. The workers in white shop coats give the customer the sense that a service professional is working on their car. The two cars on the left are being lubricated. The center post-style hoists that these cars have been lifted on allow the car to be rotated while in the air. The white circle painted on the floor indicates the clearance zone. *Copyright © 1978-1999 GM Corp. Used with permission of GM Media Archives*

To promote their accessory parts business, many dealers would outfit one of their showroom display cars with several dealer-installed accessories. Added to this 1934 Chevrolet sedan are rear wheel skirts, a driver's-side spotlight, and dual chrome horns. Behind the car is an anti-freeze display advising customers to get ready for winter.

During World War II many mechanics who had worked in dealerships went off to war. To fill the need for qualified mechanics, women readily took their places greasing cars and changing spark plugs. *FDR Library*

PARTS
ROOM
CASHIER

spoke into a microphone connected to a public address system that could be heard throughout the service area.

Up in the tower, the dispatcher maintained a master schedule sheet that served as the nerve center of the control system. From the tower, the dispatcher was able to keep the service writers advised on the status of every department in the service area through lights mounted on the front of the tower. Each service department's name was written on the front of the tower and directly below the name were green, amber, and red lights. A green light indicated that a particular department was available for work. An amber light denoted a department that had some repair bookings, but was not sold-out for the day. The service writer was to personally check with the department head prior to assigning any work to that department. A red light indicated that the

department was filled to capacity and no additional work should be scheduled. Today, the service tower has been replaced with computer-based systems. While the computers are much more efficient, they are not as impressive as looking up from the shop floor to see the various lights illuminated on the service tower.

Increasing service department traffic and customer satisfaction is the goal of every dealership. A fresh approach to customer service was successful when, in 1948, Cochran and Celli, Chevrolet's oldest dealership in California, opened its service department from 4 P.M. to midnight. They did it primarily because no other repair agencies were available to motorists during those hours. Initially, business was slow during those hours, but the dealership conducted an extensive advertising campaign and business soon mushroomed.

These two Ford parts men have stepped out from behind the counter to have their portrait taken. They are both wearing suits under their spotless white shop coats. On the wall to the left is a display of wheel trim rings and grille guards. The area above the parts room is where larger items such as fenders and axles are stored.

Showroom displays like this one at a Mercury-Zephyr dealer would entice the buyer of a new car to personalize it with a radio, spotlight, or wheel trim rings. Dealers have always loved to sell accessories because of the high profit margins they carry.

This front end aligning equipment was state of the art in 1946. Factory-trained dealership mechanics were taught how to service the new models using the latest tools and methods. *Copyright © 1978-1999 GM Corp. Used with permission of GM Media Archives*

This service department is teeming with work. Every hoist has a car and all the mechanics are busy. The roof of this service department is supported by steel trusses, which keeps the entire floor area free of pillars and makes the movement of cars easier. Also, most of the light for the area is provided by the skylights and windows. Most of the overhead lights are turned off.

The service writer's job is to quickly assess the customer's problem and give the customer an estimate of time and cost for the repairs. Many of these service writers were promoted from the ranks of mechanics because of their broad range of vehicle knowledge. *Copyright © 1978-1999 GM Corp. Used with permission of GM Media Archives*

In 1963, Cochran and Celli had a staff of 13 mechanics who worked the night shift. In addition to mechanics, the department had a shop foreman, a parts man, and a cashier. At that time, the journeyman mechanics received $3.31 per hour and an additional 10 percent shift premium. The mechanics enjoyed the night shift because the pace of work was much more relaxed. They often had a chance to discuss a specific complaint with the car's owner, which helped to resolve the problem. The dealership's owners also found that due to a closer working relationship between the mechanics and the customer, more leads were developed for the new car sales department. Because of the working conditions and additional pay, new openings were rare on the night shift.

The early 1960s saw a shortage of qualified automobile mechanics. California alone needed 10,000 mechanics. Cochran and Celli's night shift also served as the training ground for their apprentice program. Dealership president Ben Celli felt that training mechanics was one of the keys to the future of the dealership.

Selling on the floor of the service department is an important activity for the service writers of any dealership, and they use two ways to sell a customer additional

Mack-Gratiot Chevrolet in Detroit, Michigan, kept its service department open 24 hours a day. Many customers found it convenient to bring their car in for service after normal business hours. The mechanics who worked the second and third shift enjoyed the pay premium they received for working nights. *Copyright © 1978-1999 GM Corp. Used with permission of GM Media Archives*

In the 1940s, Motorola supplied radios and showroom displays to new car dealerships. This ad from a NADA Bulletin demonstrates how the radio will "sell itself."

service— "selling tools" and "motivating tools." One of the best selling tools is a regular inspection performed in front of the customer. A safety inspection is a preventative maintenance program designed to stop trouble before it starts. Even a quick inspection may reveal a need for several services that may prevent an expensive future repair or breakdown on the road. Another selling tool is a periodic review of the customer's service record, which is a consultative approach that shows the owner how to get the most value from his or her new car.

A "motivating tool" is an attractive display that shows a comparison of new and old parts to attract the customer's attention and build interest. The dealerships would often have a display promoting new brakes. The display would contain an old brake shoe with lining worn dangerously low and a new one next to it with a full lining. These displays are designed to create the desire for a product or service and to motivate the customer to buy on impulse. Another motivational tool is a special price on a component or service, which, in combination with a sales incentive for the service writer, can be exceptionally profitable for the department.

Making the service department profitable is exactly what happened in 1958 at K. A. Childs Motors in Kingsville, Texas, when they started to regularly feature two monthly service specials. One month, the specials

It wasn't until the 1960s that heaters became standard equipment on all cars. Motorola, in addition to selling radios, also sold these gasoline accessory heaters at dealer parts counters.

THE HARLEY-DAVIDSON SERVI-CAR

The Harley-Davidson Servi-Car first appeared in late 1931, available for sale with the 1932 models. Conceived and designed in the late 1920s, its concept was simple. Design a motorcycle that anyone can ride in almost any weather with space available for storage. Because of their low cost and versatility, Servi-Cars were quickly adapted by automobile service departments. In the 1930s, it wasn't unusual for a car salesman to bring a new model car out to a prospective customer's house for a firsthand look or test drive. With the Servi-Car, repair service could also be handled at home, too. The dealer's mobile mechanic would ride to the owner's home on a Servi-Car. Simple repairs were done on the spot with tools and service parts carried in the Servi-Car's spacious rear body box. If the vehicle needed to be taken to the dealership for more serious work, the mechanic would attach the Servi-Car to the car's rear bumper (Model GA was equipped with a front tow bar). The mechanic could drive the car with the handsome Servi-Car in tow. When finished servicing the car at the dealership, the mechanic would drive it back to the customer's house, unhook the Servi-Car's tow bar and motor back to the dealership. The Servi-Car's large box offered another benefit to the business owner—it provided a convenient large surface for dealer advertisement.

The forward tilting box lid was often upholstered for the comfort of the occasional passenger. Optional handles for the sides of the box were available, giving the rear passenger something to hold on to. At employee picnics, this rear box doubled as an ice chest.

The Servi-Car was designed like a tricycle and it handled like one. Most mechanics usually drove them too fast, forgetting they were on a three-wheeler. Rounding corners was a spectacle. Expecting

The Harley-Davidson Servi-Car gave customers an extra level of service. Instead of waiting in line for repairs, a smartly attired attendant would ride out to the customer's house on the dealer's Servi-Car to pick up the customer's car. The large rear box provided ample space to display the dealer's name.

Copyright © 1978-1999 GM Corp. Used with permission of GM Media Archives

The Harley-Davidson Servi-Car had a built-in tow bar. It could be quickly attached to the rear bumper of a customer's car, which gave the mechanic the option of driving the car back to the dealership, if necessary, with the Servi-Car in tow. *Copyright © Harley-Davidson*

the vehicle to behave like a two-wheeler, the rider would lean his body into the turn, but the Servi-Car doesn't lean.

The Servi-Car was simple, but well designed. Even though other three-wheeled designs were available, none were as well executed. The rear frame was a rather complex design utilizing a combination of leaf and coil springs. The rear axle was an adaptation of an automotive design with a chain drive sprocket driving both rear wheels. The Servi-Car's overall length was 100 inches and the rear tread was 42 inches. This wide tread enabled the rider to drive in auto tire paths during snowy weather. Servi-Cars were equipped with a hand-shifted, three-speed transmission with a reverse gear. The reverse gear gave the mechanic flexibility in parking and maneuvering. The engine for all Servi-Cars

was the Harley-Davidson DS-45. This 21-horsepower engine, first introduced in 1929, served faithfully on all Servi-Cars until production ceased in 1974. Technical changes over the life of the Servi-Car were few. Electric starters were introduced in 1964, and in 1966, the rear box and fenders were made of fiberglass.

Law enforcement agencies quickly adopted the Servi-Car for their use. It provided them with an all-weather utility vehicle. Most Servi-Cars were used for parking enforcement and Harley-Davidson even offered a tire marking stick as an option.

Today, Servi-Cars have been replaced by courtesy vans and tow trucks. Unfortunately, neither has the panache and distinction of a dealer mechanic coming to a customer's home to fix their car.

This Lincoln dealer has moved its accessory display out into the showroom on a wheeled cart. While the salesman is showing the new Continental Cabriolet, he can point out the comfort and convenience accessories available. *From the collections of Henry Ford Museum & Greenfield Village and Ford Motor Company*

were undercoating for $15.95 and a front-end check for $6.95, plus parts. Two large signs were placed in the service department entrance where each customer driving in could easily notice them. One of the two monthly specials was singled out for a promotional mailing to all of the dealership's service customers. The service specials were also included in the dealership's new and used car newspaper advertising. Dale Gardner, the dealership's service manager, noticed a tripling of business when a service special was promoted. This additional trade was welcomed by the service writers who each received a 5 percent commission on all service department business. It also helped expand the service business in general by acquainting more car owners with the dealership's service department. Many of those first-time service customers soon became regulars.

Rendering quality service to the customer is the mission of any dealership service department. This goodwill is an intangible asset that cannot be accurately

Maintaining an adequate supply of parts for the dealership's mechanics, retail, and wholesale customers is an ongoing process. Here, the parts manager, in the crisp shop coat, is checking an inventory sheet with the owner. The space needed for a dealership parts department is typically 10 percent of the total floor space.

The dealership parts department is designed to service the customer with factory-approved parts. The items range from regular replacement parts, such as spark plugs, knee-action shock absorbers, and batteries, to vehicle-specific items such as grilles, bumpers, and chrome trim.

On any given day, a myriad of repairs is simultaneously being performed within a dealership service department. On the far right, a technician is demonstrating to the customer a piece of electronic tune-up equipment. In the foreground, a service writer is writing up a repair order. Behind him, a mechanic is about to get behind the wheel of a sedan to deliver it to the owner's home. Attached to the rear bumper of that sedan is a Harley-Davidson Servi-Car that the mechanic will ride back to the dealership. On the far left, a car is up on a lift being lubricated. In the background, each service bay has a car in some state of repair.

Copyright © 1978-1999 GM Corp. Used with permission of GM Media Archives

measured in dollars and cents, but poor customer service will most certainly ruin any dealership. The dealership needs and depends on satisfied customers, but the customers neither need nor depend on a single dealership. The customer flatters a dealership when a vehicle is brought in for work. The dealer cannot jeopardize this source of income by careless or inconsiderate treatment of the customer. A satisfied service customer will return to buy new cars and continue to use the dealership's service department for regular vehicle maintenance. Satisfied customers influence their friends and relatives. That's the way service reputations are made.

Parts and Service in Action

Throughout the 1950s and 1960s, Americans hit the roads like never before. The network of interstate highways was falling in place and the family automobile was the preferred method of travel. In 1961, Americans made more than 215 million vacation or pleasure trips—drives that were more than 100 miles from home or required an overnight stay—by car. In fact, 90 percent of all domestic vacations in the early 1960s were by car. At that time, America's annual vacation budget was $20 billion. To tap into this vast potential, many automobile dealer service departments offered seasonal specials to their customers, something gasoline service stations had

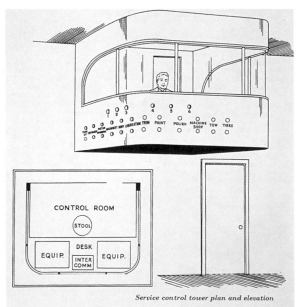

Service control tower plan and elevation

The clever marketing staff at Packard figured Christmas was as good a time as any to promote accessories. This well-heeled lady is in a Packard showroom looking at the "This Christmas Give Packard Accessories" display. On it is a spotlight for "dad," tilt-type mirror for "sis," a vanity mirror for "mom," and exhaust pipe trim for "brother." *Ken Stevens collection*

Dealers with large service departments would often have a control tower that maintained an overview of the floor. On the exterior of the towers, lights indicated to the service writers which departments were available for assignments.

Along the back wall of this Kaiser-Frazer service department is the parts counter and cashier. This dealership was also a Goodyear tire retailer. The mezzanine above the parts department provided storage for the stock of tires.
Charlie DiBari collection

The service entrance to this Pontiac dealership is lined with circular and radiused windows reminisent of Art Deco themes. Wainscot is the treatment of an interior wall where the lower two or three feet are finished differently from the rest of the wall. The lower portion of these walls appears to be metal panels that would be durable and easy to clean. On the far end of the left wall is the parts counter.
Escondido Historical Society

By the late 1940s, the hardware store style of parts display had given way to clean modern parts counters. The customer had to depend on the expertise of the counter employee. Behind the counter, this dealership has built some interesting geometric parts display windows. *Copyright © 1978-1999 GM Corp. Used with permission of GM Media Archives*

been regularly doing for years. Just when motorists were dusting off their ice chests and picnic baskets and thinking about hitting the road for the time-honored summer vacation, the smart service manager was planning how to increase dealer profit and customer satisfaction.

The first step was to convince the dealer's regular customers of the necessity for safe, dependable, and economical transportation during vacation periods. The strategy was to offer the customer more than a tune-up and an oil change when they came in for service. A complete safety check was offered that took only minutes to do, but that often sold other important services

to the customer. A quick check of the cooling system might detect a faulty hose that could fail, stranding the customer on the road. Road maps, tourist guides, and lists of attractions were freely given to vacation-bound customers. Giving the customer the name and address of the local dealer at a vacation destination gave the motorist comfort in knowing where repairs could be made on the road. A checklist of necessary vacation reminders cost little for the dealer to prepare, but added a touch of thoughtfulness. The dealer's parts department offered specials on emergency kits and road flares and would even throw in a game or comic book to keep

AUTO ACCESSORIES OVER THE YEARS

In the mid 1930s, automobile dealers and manufacturers realized that customers were looking for more than a motorized black box to transport them along the roads. Bright two-tone colors were fashionable and so was the addition of accessories to the car. As the year wore on, many of the accessories that were formerly bought over the parts counter became standard equipment and others were no longer needed (goggles, for instance). Selling accessories had always been profitable for the dealer. The following three lists contain dealer accessories from 1938, 1958, and 1998.

1938	1958	1998
Awnings	Back-up lamp	18-inch alloy wheels
Assist cords	Continental	with Z-rated tires
Bumper jacks	wheel carrier	Aerodynamic body pieces
Clock	Seat covers	Theft alarm systems
Curtains	Door edge guard	CD decks
Driving lights	Door handle shield	Driving lights
Fender skirts	Dummy antenna	Floor mats
Goggles	Electric clock	Suspension kits
Heaters	Exhaust port	
Radiator caps	Illuminated compass	
Seat covers	Rear seat speaker	
Spotlights	Seat belts	
Steering knobs	Vacuum ashtray	
Tire covers	Wheel cover spinners	
Telephones		
Windshield wipers		

When the Edsel was introduced, Ford Motor Company attempted to build a visual identity for its dealers. All Edsel signs were green and white in color, with the letter "E" enclosed in a circle. *From the collections of Ford Motor Company*

the kids quiet in the back seat while on the road. A little inventive thinking by the service staff would keep the service lanes filled year-round. It also bolstered the service department's business and profits.

The accessory business is good from a profit standpoint. Because little price cutting is involved, the profit margins are high. Dealers found out that it took little effort to sell most accessories. For display, dealers used the "five and dime" method of putting everything out in the open for the potential customer to see and avoided the hard sell.

Many dealers would load their demo cars with every accessory the parts department had to offer. When the salespeople gave new car prospects a test drive, they could show them the benefit of each accessory. Soon potential customers would see the extras as necessities and would ask for them on the car they'd eventually purchase.

In the mid 1950s, dealers came to recognize that half of all service department business was purchased by women. In an effort to seize that market, the Alemite Company, then a division of Stewart Warner, came up with a series of seminars for car dealers called "Gas, Gaskets, and Glamour." The Alemite folks provided all the materials to any dealer wanting to conduct a seminar. The plan was for the seminars to help dealers gain the women as customers by teaching them a little about what made their car tick. The Alemite Company even showed the dealer how to get free publicity when hold-

You can almost hear the owner of this Oldsmobile saying to the service writer, "I know that rattle is coming from back here." Often the best way to convey the extent of a problem is to get the car up on a hoist and let the customer see for himself the cause of the problem. *Courtesy Oldsmobile History Center*

ing one of these schools. The response was outstanding. One dealer in New York City drew 448 women over a two-week period. Another in California hosted over 200 women in 10 days.

The first automobile manufacturers were aware that to properly support their customers, they had to provide service and parts. The dealers found that these components added two extra profit centers to their business. They also found out that the lack of an efficient service department hurt the sales of new cars. These dealers realized that the buyers enjoyed personalizing their new cars by adding accessories. By developing the "back end" of the business, the most successful and profitable dealers have stayed that way.

BIBLIOGRAPHY

Books

American Automobile Manufacturers Association, Inc. *Automobiles of America*. Sidney, OH: Cars & Parts Magazine, 1996.

Dominguez, Henry. *The Ford Agency*. Osceola, WI: Motorbooks International, 1981.

Eskeldson, Mark. *What Car Dealers Don't Want You to Know*. Fair Oaks, CA: 1995.

Finch, Christopher. *Highways to Heaven*. New York: Harper Collins, 1992.

General Motors, *Planning Automobile Dealership Properties*. General Motors, 1948.

Halberstam, David. *The Reckoning*. New York: William Avon, 1986.

Holder, William. *The Automobile Dealer: Yesterday, Today and Tomorrow*. NADA, 1957.

Ingrassia, Paul & Joseph B. White. *Comeback, The Fall and Rise of the American Automobile Industry*. New York: Simon & Schuster, 1994.

Mantle, Jonathan. *Car Wars*. New York: Arcade, 1996

Sobel, Robert. *Car Wars*. New York: E.P. Dutton, 1984.

Yates, Brock. *The Decline and Fall of the American Automobile Industry*. New York: Empire, 1983.

Magazine and Periodical Articles

"Action in Used Car Sales." *NADA Magazine* (January 1955).

"Automobile Incentives—A Backward Glance." *Wheels* (Summer/Fall 1998).

"Bidding at Auction." *Motor Trend* (June 1965).

"A Code for Indiana." *NADA Magazine* (October 1958).

"Dodge's Charter Dealers." *WPC News* (November 1998).

"The Edsel Car—Was It a Bomb or a Boon?" *Automotive News* (June 1978).

"Emphasis on Women." *NADA Magazine* (October 1955).

"Far-Reaching Effects of the 'Truth-In-Labeling' Law." *NADA Magazine* (October 1959).

"The Franchiser Foundation." *Automotive Executive* (May 1992).

"Glass Showrooms Lure Customers." *NADA Magazine* (August 1963).

"Hoe-Down Hauls Up Sales." *NADA Magazine* (September 1959).

"Hottest Cars on the Lot." *Motor Trend* (June 1966).

"In the Beginning." *Automotive Executive* (May 1992).

"Industry Junking Plan a Necessity." *NADA Bulletin* (February 1938).

"Liven Up Your Showroom." *NADA Magazine* (June 1964).

"A Love-Hate Relationship." *Automotive Executive* (May 1992).

"Movers and Shakers." *Automotive Executive* (May 1992).

"My Own Page." *The Accelerator* (February 1927).

"The NADA Story." *Automotive Executive* (May 1992).

"NADA'S 75th Anniversary Special." *Automotive Executive* (May 1992).

"New Models—New Sales." *NADA Magazine* (September 1959).

"Nighttime Is the Right Time." *NADA Magazine* (May 1963).

"Plan Would Junk Worn-out Used Cars Systematically." *NADA Bulletin* (February 1938).

"Planned Prospecting Pays off at Hodges." *NADA Magazine* (October 1958).

"Playing by the Rules." *Automotive Executive* (May 1992).

"Profit Possibilities in Open Display of Accessories." *NADA Bulletin* (December 1938).

"A Seasonal Journey into Profits." *NADA Magazine* (June 1963).

"Sell on Sight." *NADA Magazine* (October 1962).

"Shine Up Used Car Displays." *NADA Magazine* (June 1964).

" 'Show Me' Week Big Success." *The Accelerator* (July 1928).

"Single Point Stores, Megadealer Mania." *Automotive Executive* (May 1992).

"Six Thousand Prospects." *NADA Magazine* (April 1955).

"Special Event Promotions." *NADA Magazine* (September 1959).

"Standing the Test of Time." *PRO* (February 1998).

"Tales of a Retail Pioneer." *Automotive News* (March 1999).

"Wanted! An Industry Junking Program." *NADA Bulletin* (January 1938).

"The Warranty War." *Motor Trend* (June 1965).

INDEX